home TRULY

BUILDING DREAMS, HOUSING HOPES

HOUSING & DEVELOPMENT BOARD

CONTENTS

> "Many future generations of Singaporeans will continue to grow up in HDB townships, and their collective experiences will continue to be a major part of our national identity."

FOREWORD

SINGAPOREANS and visitors are familiar with our spectacular city skyline – the iconic buildings at Marina Bay, the central business district, and the Singapore Flyer. But further north in Punggol is another equally breathtaking skyline, with verdant greenery, beautiful waterways, and distinctive districts.

Punggol was the first Housing and Development Board (HDB) project that reflected its ambition to build vibrant, sustainable, and affordable public housing estates. Since then, HDB has developed Bidadari, a lush, thriving HDB estate that is close to completion, and is starting to develop Tengah, our first smart and sustainable town.

As HDB marks its 60th anniversary, it can look back proudly at these and many more accomplishments, while planning ahead for new possibilities for public housing in Singapore.

When we first began our public housing journey 60 years ago, things were very different. Fewer than 10 percent of Singaporeans owned a home, and many lived in crowded and squalid conditions. The then newly elected PAP government established HDB and gave it the urgent task of building as many low-cost units as quickly as possible. It succeeded, and by the 1970s, our severe housing shortage had largely been overcome.

After Singapore became independent in 1965, the Government continued to promote home ownership as a fundamental policy to give Singaporeans a tangible personal stake to defend, and a share of the new country's success. In addition to the Home Ownership for the People Scheme, flat owners could, starting from 1968, use their Central Provident Fund savings to pay for HDB flats. This brought home ownership within the reach of most Singaporeans.

Subsequently, to meet the aspirations of a younger, more educated generation, HDB began to build bigger flats with better designs and finishes, and introduced major upgrading and renewal programmes for the older estates to bring them close to the standards of the newer ones.

Today, eight in 10 Singaporeans live in HDB flats, and nine in 10 of these own the flat they live in. No other country in the world has such an extensive public housing system, and few have as high a proportion of flat owners as Singapore.

As our society matures, HDB will have to continue to make public housing attractive to Singaporeans, and address their changing needs and rising expectations. HDB will have to take into account not just the tangible aspects like sustainability, energy efficiency, and transport connectivity, but also the intangible ones like heritage and community interests.

These layers transform an HDB flat into a home, because a home is more than four walls – it is where experiences are shared and memories made, where families forge deep ties and communities flourish. This way, many future generations of Singaporeans will continue to grow up in HDB townships, and their collective experiences will continue to be a major part of our national identity.

I wish HDB every success as it celebrates its 60th anniversary.

Lee Hsien Loong
Prime Minister

MESSAGE FROM LAWRENCE WONG

"Over the past 60 years, the Housing and Development Board's (HDB) meticulous efforts to plan, build, and continually improve public housing in Singapore has led to where we are today, where homes are beautiful in both function and form."

THIS is not without challenges. The past decade has been especially daunting for HDB, as it grappled with a volatile economy that impacted the property market, continually changing lifestyles, and rising expectations.

HDB successfully navigated those challenges while maintaining a steadfast focus on the needs of Singaporeans. It has held fast to its core, evergreen mission: To keep public housing affordable and accessible for all Singaporeans.

Housing grants have been enhanced to ensure that home ownership always remains within reach, especially for young couples setting up their first home. A typical first-timer family can service their monthly mortgage instalments with less than 25 percent of their monthly income, and with little or no cash outlay.

Apart from keeping flats affordable, I also set HDB a challenge to help Singaporeans get their homes faster. HDB has more than delivered.

Virtually all first-timer families have been successful within their first three tries for a Build-To-Order flat in a non-mature estate. HDB has launched projects with a shorter waiting time of between two and three years, as well as a new sales mode – the open booking of flats – which allows buyers with urgent needs to apply online for a flat at almost any time of the year and select a flat as early as the next working day.

Another key aspect of HDB's work is sustaining the liveability of our HDB estates. This requires deliberate long-term planning, and HDB has invested heavily in renewing and upgrading our existing housing estates to ensure they remain good places to live regardless of age. In just the past five years, close to $3 billion has been spent on our various upgrading programmes.

In all of this, what is clear is that Singapore's public housing journey is an ongoing one. There is always more to be done.

That gave HDB a strong impetus to come up with its Roadmap to Better Living in HDB Towns to guide the development of well-designed, sustainable and smart, and community-centric towns. With the Roadmap, HDB went on to develop projects you are familiar with – Punggol Point District, Punggol Northshore, Bidadari, Kampung Admiralty, and Tengah. Many of the projects have won local and international awards, testament to the high quality of HDB's planning, research, and design efforts.

Home, Truly aims to capture HDB's commitment to providing a good quality environment and beautiful abodes.

Through interviews with past and present HDB staff, it offers a deep dive into the thinking behind the shift in HDB's approach to public housing, the critical decisions it had to make, and how the Roadmap continues to evolve and shape HDB living going into the future.

Conversations with external partners and residents who were part of the last decade of transformation, too, add to a story that is built not just on HDB's good work, but also on the collaborative effort of the community.

Beyond just providing a shelter for Singaporeans, HDB's role has evolved to building homes and communities. In the last chapter of this book, residents share their own heartfelt stories of what HDB living means to them – be it a nest to start a family, a space for friends and loved ones to gather, or a sanctuary to seek comfort and refuge – and is a reminder of why HDB does what it does.

This year, HDB turns 60 amid challenging times. With the COVID-19 pandemic, HDB living has taken on a new meaning, and the comfort and familiarity of our homes become more crucial to engender resilience among citizens.

HDB's work never ends, and I am confident it will only get better. I look forward to seeing HDB living continue to flourish as HDB celebrates many more milestones in the future.

Lawrence Wong
Minister for National Development (2015 – 2020)

MESSAGE FROM DESMOND LEE

"When I spoke at the launch of the HDB Community Week at Kampung Admiralty in 2019, I was struck by how the integrated development had grown into its own, bringing our vision of developing a high-rise *kampung* (Malay for 'village') into reality."

FITTED with a full range of facilities and amenities that promote active living and inter-generational bonding, Kampung Admiralty has become a place where residents of all ages can bond over many activities – from exercising and gardening, to cooking and sharing a meal. It is a place where strong community ties are forged, and where neighbours step in to a lend a hand to those who need help.

In a modern *kampung* like this, it is all about relationships and building trust.

The Housing and Development Board's (HDB) success in creating initiatives to improve neighbourhoods and strengthen communities is underpinned by its close working relationships with residents, grassroots, and the larger community, which it has sustained over the decades. I got to see this in action when I joined the Ministry of National Development in 2013.

This ethos of community and partnership – Singapore Together – will be even more relevant as we move into the future. We want to get more Singaporeans involved in our plans.

In particular, we want to involve residents at the early stages of projects including in design and planning. This will give residents a larger stake in their estate, and a greater sense of ownership of common spaces.

In fact, we have already prototyped the participative design processes in Tampines in 2015, under the Hello Neighbour! @ Tampines Central project. Over 10 months, more than 1,000 residents participated in focus group discussions, in-depth interviews, and design workshops to share their views and suggestions on how social spaces could be re-designed and used to facilitate community bonding.

The residents came together and transformed an empty void deck into a cosy community café that also functions as a community library. In fact, residents are now making use of these new spaces for their regular breakfast and exercise sessions as well.

For the Remaking Our Heartland programme, HDB has been actively engaging the community by inviting residents and community stakeholders to brainstorm ideas and co-create plans to rejuvenate their towns through focus group discussions. We will carry on doing so for future proposals. We will also continue to engage nature and heritage groups during the planning process to conserve our rich biodiversity and heritage, where possible.

Anyone with good ideas on how to make our housing estates livelier and more vibrant can also tap on the Lively Places Programme, which funds and facilitates ground-up initiatives. Co-creation and partnership have been and will continue to be a key part of how we work, because we want to give every Singaporean a role in shaping our future city and home.

As Singapore progresses, we will conscientiously ensure that public housing remains accessible to all and look out for the interests of our vulnerable groups, such as our seniors and low-income families, to guide them towards attaining a stable home. For example, through the Home ownership Support Team, we will further our partnership with various agencies to provide personalised support to families living in public rental flats as they progress towards home ownership.

Building caring communities and championing gracious heartland living is HDB's way of life. We will continue to nurture a corps of passionate volunteers – our Friends of Our Heartlands volunteers and HDB alumni – who will uphold these values. Singapore's housing landscape is quite unlike anywhere else in the world. We live in high-rise buildings in a dense urban city, yet there is no lack of the *kampung* spirit that binds Singaporeans together.

All of these would not have been possible without the solid foundations laid by our pioneers, such as HDB's first chairman, Mr Lim Kim San. That good work has carried on through the years under the charge of various leaders including my predecessors Mr Khaw Boon Wan and Mr Lawrence Wong. I would also like to thank HDB staff, both past and present, for their hard work and for making Singapore's housing journey possible.

HDB marks its 60th anniversary this year. Through each of the past six decades, HDB has evolved from providing basic housing solutions to becoming the world leader in building sustainable, affordable, and well-designed homes and communities for Singaporeans. As HDB embarks on its seventh decade, we can look forward to its refreshed roadmap, 'Designing for Life', which will help pave the way for future HDB living. There is so much more we can build on, and so much more we can do to jointly create plans to refresh and enliven our community spaces.

Desmond Lee
Minister for National Development (2020 – present)

CHAPTER 1

ROADMAP TO BETTER LIVING

A DECADE OF TRANSFORMATION

Bata

“Lifestyles change, aspirations change, and we have to keep up with the times. What's wonderful about this is that we can do new things. It was an opportunity to create a whole new generation of public housing.”

Dr Cheong Koon Hean
Chief Executive Officer

When the Housing and Development Board (HDB) was set up in 1960, there was an urgency to resolve Singapore's severe housing shortage – by turning squatter settlements into new sanctuaries of high-rise flats and communities.

Over time, HDB progressed from simply providing a roof over residents' heads to pushing new frontiers in public housing, designing stunning yet sustainable skyscraper flats and liveable towns.

If the building plan 60 years ago had dramatically altered Singapore's public housing landscape, which continued to evolve through the years, the changes in the last decade were equally transformative for the modern metropolis.

In 2010, Singapore was on the cusp of a new challenge. This time, it was the hot property market born out of the swift economic recovery after the 2008 Global Financial Crisis.

As demand for new flats surged, HDB sprang into action and increased the flat supply significantly. Between 2011 and 2014, HDB launched almost 100,000 Build-To-Order (BTO) flats, which helped to restore the balance in demand and supply.

As HDB ramped up the supply of new flats, it also grasped the golden opportunity to do something different – to build a new generation of homes and towns that not only catered to changing aspirations, but was also sustainable and brought the community closer together.

At the heart of the plan was a roadmap, which offered a blueprint to guide HDB's development programme for the next one to two decades.

Unveiled in November 2011, the Roadmap to Better Living in HDB Towns comprised three thrusts in developing towns: well-designed, sustainable and smart, and community-centric.

With this, HDB, the master planner and developer of homes and towns, not only sculpts HDB towns into sustainable housing communities, but also renews older towns into liveable spaces.

This is what sets HDB apart from other public housing providers in other countries. As HDB has chronicled its first 50 years in an earlier publication, the following pages tell the story of how HDB overcame the challenges of the last 10 years.

The HDB story – from 1960 till today

IT was the 1950s and Singapore did not have sufficient homes for its swelling population. The number of residents had increased dramatically following the Second World War, jumping 50 percent in 10 years – from 938,144 in 1947 to 1,445,926 in 1957.

Yet, the development of new permanent housing units lagged behind the demographic growth. The Singapore Improvement Trust (SIT), which was set up in 1927 for general improvement works, took on the additional role of providing low-cost public housing to alleviate the overcrowding problem in the city centre of Singapore in the 1930s. In total, SIT built close to 23,000 flats over a period of 32 years – significantly below the number that the population needed.

As a result, squatter huts and shacks sprouted across Singapore, from Siglap to Telok Blangah, to house the growing number of residents and quell the rising demand for accommodation.

It was against this backdrop that HDB was set up in 1960, with an urgent task to build more housing units and relocate people from unhygienic squatter houses to decent homes fitted with modern sanitation.

By 1965, HDB delivered by completing 54,430 units under its first Five-Year Building Programme. It was well on its way to solving the acute housing crisis.

The new flats changed the face of Singapore. Instead of unsightly slums, villages, and wastelands, the landscape was now predominantly made up of neat rows of multi-storeyed blocks that clustered to form neighbourhoods with schools, shopping centres, clinics, and playgrounds.

Today, HDB has contributed to the Singapore success story, offering citizens a stake in the country with its home ownership policies, as well as impressive and inspiring new-generation homes that cater to changing lifestyles.

by **1965**
HDB had completed
54,430 units

from **1947** to **1957**,
the number of residents had increased significantly from
938,144 ▸ 1,445,926

A new block of HDB flats in Ellenborough Street stands out among pre-war shopehouses in 1974.

TOP: High-rise HDB flats in the Redhill / Henderson redevelopment area in 1971.

BOTTOM: HDB introduced the Home Ownership for the People Scheme in 1964.

THE 2010 HOUSING CONUNDRUM

TO understand the housing shortage at the turn of the last decade requires a retracing of steps into the 1990s.

Back then, Singapore enjoyed a period of sustained and robust economic growth, which led to a rise in resale property prices and strong demand for new flats. At one point, there were as many as 150,000 buyers in the public housing queue[1], and the wait took as long as seven years.

But the demand vanished almost overnight when the Asian Financial Crisis struck in 1997, with the number of flat applications dropping to a low of just over 7,000 in 1998.

While Singapore's growth rebounded in 1999, another crisis emerged a year later – the dot-com collapse in 2000 that sent the economy into a recession. Against the backdrop of these two crises, HDB spent about five years clearing its overhang of 31,000 flats.

To prevent an unintended oversupply from occurring again, a new Build-To-Order (BTO) System was implemented in 2002, following a successful pilot a year earlier. HDB would start building new flats only when seven out of 10 units have been booked by interested buyers.

1 The Registration for Flat System was a queue system that allowed applicants to apply for a unit in their preferred zone and be allocated a flat based on their queue position.

Three precincts in Sembawang were the first projects launched under the Build-To-Order sales exercise.

Waterway Sunbeam

The new system, coupled with other measures from HDB, helped to ease the property glut by 2006. But barely two years later in 2008, the world was rocked by the Global Financial Crisis – a severe global recession ignited by the subprime mortgage problems in the United States. Singapore was among the first few countries in East Asia to slide into recession.

HDB was cautious not to over-build flats ahead of demand. This time, however, the downturn was short-lived as countries responded quickly with massive stimulus packages.

Singapore was no different. In the first half of 2010, its Gross Domestic Product posted a year-on-year growth of 18 percent.

The strong recovery and low interest rate environment played a part in improving sentiments and reducing the cost of property financing. Backed by demographics, the demand surged in both the public and private housing markets in Singapore. In fact, the demand for flats rebounded so strongly that there were not enough new flats. Many buyers then turned to the resale market, driving up prices of resale flats.

There was a need to relook at the provision of public housing and chart a new path forward.

in **2002**, the

BTO System

was implemented

THE GREAT CONSTRUCTION

IT was clear to HDB that it had to boost its supply of flats. It set out to quickly ramp up the building programme for BTO flats. The entire organisation was mobilised to achieve this turbo-charged construction schedule.

The planners first secured approval for the master plan relating to new development areas like Tampines North, Punggol Northshore, Punggol Point District, and Tengah, where they would build new flats. Multi-disciplinary teams of consultants came on board, and the architects and engineers oversaw designs for infrastructure and building projects, all while ensuring there was adequate supply of building materials and components, and maintaining the quality of flats. Precinct by precinct, blueprints were transformed into homes.

“Despite the increased workload, HDB staff rallied together and worked tirelessly towards the common goal to increase the supply of HDB flats and serve our customers.”

Mr Michael Koh
President of the HDB Staff Union

Builders using prefabrication technology in the construction process.

HDB's upgrading of older flats also picked up steam, as it sought to make sure that existing towns and estates could enjoy a quality living environment that was similar to the newer developments. At the same time, new policies were introduced and existing ones were reviewed to ensure public housing remained affordable and accessible.

It was a trying period but HDB staff were motivated and worked hard, recalled Mr Michael Koh, President of the HDB Staff Union.

Construction works in Punggol post-2000.

Building more flats, faster

A significant policy shift was to develop more BTO flats, ahead of demand. It was a departure from the usual approach since the system began in 2002.

In 2011, about 25,000 BTO units were launched, up from about 16,000 units in 2010, and about 9,000 units in 2009.

On top of the above, HDB announced about 2,900 flats as replacement flats for units that underwent the Selective En bloc Redevelopment Scheme (SERS).

All this was done in a carefully calibrated manner, to avoid ending up with too many unsold units.

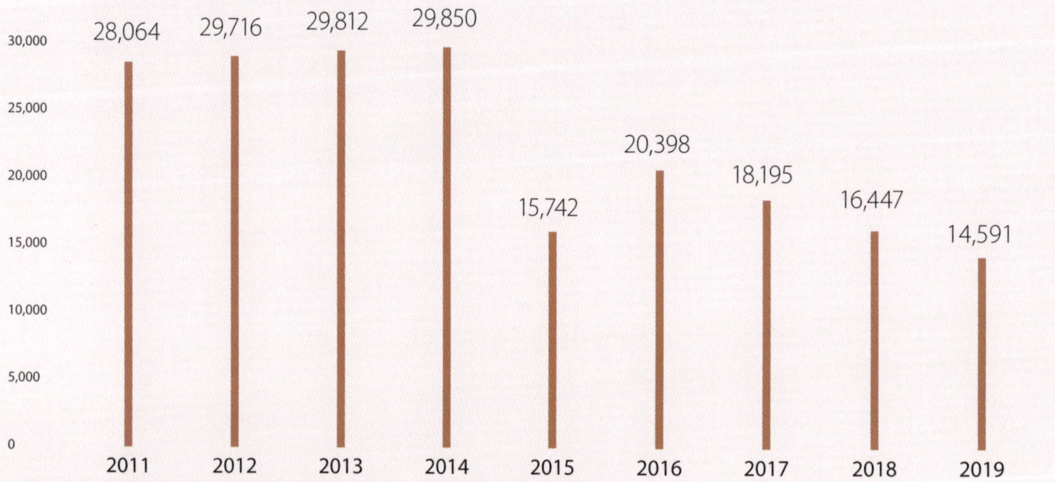

NUMBER OF DWELLING UNITS* LAUNCHED THROUGH THE YEARS

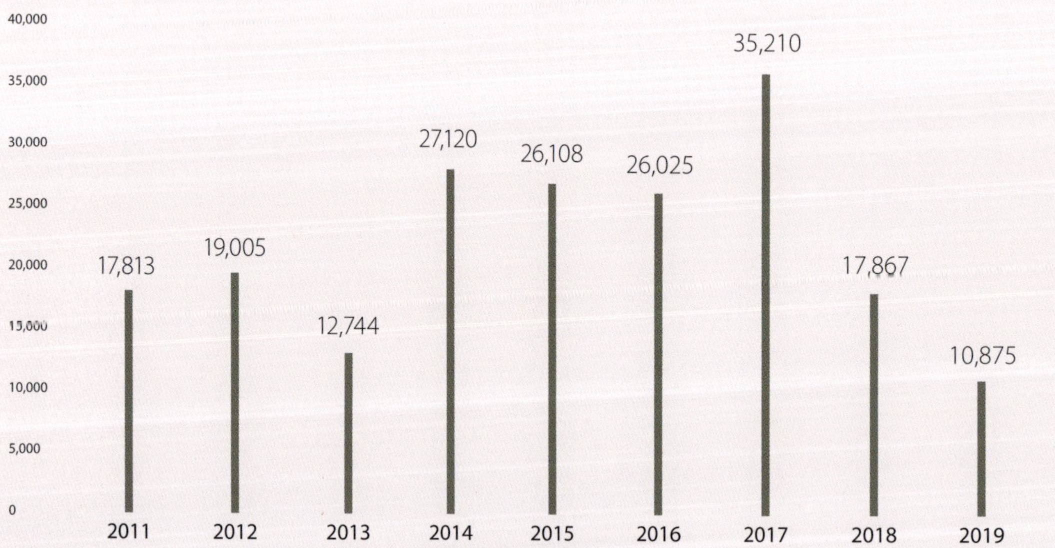

NUMBER OF DWELLING UNITS* COMPLETED THROUGH THE YEARS

*The number of dwelling units in both graphs are made up of BTO flats, SERS replacement flats, and rental flats.

Trepidation… and then a soft landing

TREPIDATION and expectation. This was the phrase that former Minister Khaw Boon Wan, known for his straight-talking ways, had chosen to describe his emotions when he took over the National Development portfolio in 2011.

In fact, he had used it as the title of his first post on Housing Matters, a blog he started to share his thoughts and document his journey in the Ministry of National Development (MND).

"Housing is hot politically and there are genuine problems on the ground," Mr Khaw wrote in the blog post on 26 May 2011, where he outlined his next steps – to focus on the housing needs of young couples, divorcees with children, and low-income families.

In the next four years, he worked with the ministry and HDB to revamp policies, enhance assistance schemes, step up HDB's building programme, and test new designs that could improve the lives of residents.

Together, they solved the housing crisis.

In September 2015, Mr Khaw signed off from his blog with a last post titled 'Phew, a much welcome soft landing'.

Summing up his time in MND, he noted that almost 100,000 new flats had been launched, with many keys handed over to new flat owners. **"The hot housing market is soft-landing nicely. But there remains much to do,"** he wrote.

Under Mr Khaw's watch, HDB had introduced new initiatives such as the 2-room Flexi Scheme aimed at helping seniors buy flats with shorter leases. It also broke new ground by allowing single citizens, aged 35 and above, to buy new 2-room HDB flats in non-mature estates.

Former Minister for National Development Mr Khaw Boon Wan and HDB CEO Dr Cheong Koon Hean at a block handover ceremony for Compassvale Ancilla in 2014. L-R: Executive Director of Ho Lee Construction Pte Ltd, Mr Micheal Tan, Mr Khaw, Dr Cheong, Group Director (Building Quality) Mr Neo Poh Kok.

THREE THRUSTS OF THE ROADMAP

THE accelerated building programme gave HDB the chance to reimagine public housing and do something different. It crafted a new vision for the homes and neighbourhoods of the future.

Guiding the vision were three broad thrusts that were distilled into the Roadmap to Better Living in HDB Towns: **well-designed, sustainable and smart, and community-centric**.

The Roadmap would enable HDB **"to deliver a better living environment and meet the evolving lifestyle aspirations of our residents,"** said its Chief Executive Officer, Dr Cheong Koon Hean, at the event to announce the Roadmap in 2011.

The Pinnacle@Duxton – An award-winning development completed in 2009.

1 DESIGN FOCUS

Over the years, HDB has regularly reviewed and updated the design of towns to keep pace with population trends and lifestyle changes.

Public housing in the 1960s was modest, as the pressing need then was moving people out of squatter settlements and into decent homes. The first HDB flats were typically built in functional slab blocks with 1- to 3-room layouts, and fitted with basic amenities such as piped water and electricity.

As Singapore progressed, residents had higher expectations. Correspondingly, HDB built larger homes, such as the 4- and 5-room flats, and introduced point blocks that offered residents more privacy. It also developed distinct identities and unique design features for new towns, and introduced better facilities such as suburban malls and thematic playgrounds.

Changes cascaded to block configurations as well. While older flats featured windows that lined common corridors, younger flat owners appreciated privacy. Hence, windows were reoriented and placed along the façade, giving residents peace, quiet, and a view of the surroundings.

Today, HDB towns are even more sophisticated with new building typologies that go beyond slab or point blocks. Some of the new blocks are much taller too, going as high as 50 storeys, with sky terraces and roof gardens providing new recreational spaces.

The 50-storey The Pinnacle@Duxton, for instance, is made up of seven towers connected by two skybridges that form a jogging track. The development features playgrounds, fitness corners, gardens, and community plazas.

The newer towns also offer a greater mix of flat types within each block and development, providing more choices to flat owners from various demographic groups and with different budgets. All towns are integrated with extensive greenery and blue elements, such as gardens, ponds, and streams, that relieve urban density.

8 principles of well-designed towns

THE eight principles guide efforts across the six focus areas outlined in the Roadmap: Greenery, Mobility & Transport, Integrated Commercial Facilities, Community, Smart & Sustainable, and Heritage.

- **Inclusion of green and blue spaces**
- **Focus on quality urban design**
- **New building typologies**
- **An environment for all ages**
- **Distinctive identities for neighbourhoods and districts**
- **New layouts for new lifestyles**
- **Car-lite environment**
- **Creating synergies from integrated developments**

The evolving kitchen concept

TO see how lifestyles have changed over the years, just look at the new kitchen layouts.

In the past, residents had to walk through the kitchen to get to the washroom. The kitchen was also the dining room and the place to hang laundry.

But not anymore. As preferences, attitudes, and lifestyles evolved, HDB responded by updating its designs of homes. The current floorplan of an HDB unit looks vastly different from past iterations.

In homes today, the washroom has been shifted out of the kitchen, and a new dining room created. For 4-room and larger flats, a separate service yard was introduced.

In the newer flats, based on feedback especially from younger buyers, the wall between the kitchen and dining room was removed, creating an open-plan area with a spacious feel. This provides flat owners with the flexibility to integrate the kitchen, living, and dining areas into a large space with a unified aesthetic. These changes suit the lifestyle of younger-generation residents who do not cook as often but enjoy entertaining friends at home.

Elaborating on how lifestyle impacts design, CEO Dr Cheong Koon Hean shared: **"Increasingly, HDB is providing 'flexi flat' layouts: where residents can fit out their flats based on their preferences and creativity."**

With the open kitchen concept, the kitchen flows into the dining space, providing flexibility for interior design.

The Verandah @ Matilda offers residents green spaces for recreational activities.

DESIGN RELIEVES DENSITY

It is easy to take comfort and convenience for granted. But a considerable amount of effort goes into deciding where certain infrastructure should be located.

In HDB towns, high- and low-rise buildings are planned thoughtfully to mitigate the high-density environment, creating a sense of spaciousness for residents. Sheltered walkways, underpasses, and overhead pedestrian bridges also shield residents from the heat.

A look at Punggol Town, which comprises seven waterfront housing districts, illustrates several key ideas of a well-designed town.

At Waterway Terraces, the distinctive terraced typology means more flat owners can enjoy the view of the man-made waterway from their homes. The development, which was inspired by the terraced rice fields of Southeast Asia, also features extensive green roofs and terraced roof gardens.

Over at Punggol Matilda, the district features open lawns and dense tree groves – a design inspired by the tropical fruit orchard that surrounded the area in the past. Such green spaces offer residents of all age groups ample green spaces to run around, read, or simply relax.

The terrain of the area also informed the design. The level difference between the waterway and the existing road presented HDB the opportunity to neatly tuck the car parks under the slope.

This move enabled the housing districts to be integrated seamlessly with the waterway, giving residents access to wide, car-free spaces. By leveraging the terrain, HDB avoided the high cost of building underground parking lots or allocating valuable land space to multi-storey car parks.

Residents gather to enjoy the living environment.

Enhancing the town design: Six focus areas

AS part of the Roadmap, HDB identified six areas that would shape towns and communities, going beyond designing within the four walls of a flat.

GREENERY

An even greater abundance of greenery, guided by biophilic principles, is now weaved into the town. Linear green corridors are layered on for improved connectivity, jogging, and cycling. Water bodies are creatively formed not only to meet functional drainage requirements, but also to complement the landscape, thereby contributing to biodiversity and adding to the recreational features of the town. Such green and blue spaces form a natural urban ecosystem, enabling residents to connect with nature.

MOBILITY & TRANSPORT

In line with the city's new push to become a car-lite society, HDB collaborates with other government agencies to encourage the use of public transport, and walk and ride modes. Towns are designed with pedestrian-friendly footpaths and cycling networks that link to parks, while park connectors promote walking and cycling. All together, these efforts encourage an active and healthy lifestyle.

INTEGRATED COMMERCIAL FACILITIES

In 2015, HDB introduced a new generation of Neighbourhood Centres (NCs) that are more than just commercial hubs for retail and dining outlets. They provide a variety of social, communal, and recreational facilities for the residents.

NCs are built to provide spaces, such as sheltered community plazas and community clubs, for activities and casual interaction. NCs are also well-linked to their surrounding housing precincts and amenities. Some are directly connected to public transport nodes.

The Punggol Waterway encapsulates the six focus areas of enhancing town design.

COMMUNITY

Community spaces play an important role in promoting social interaction and forging community bonds among residents. HDB's new towns and estates are planned with a wide variety of community spaces ranging from town plazas and common green spaces to community living rooms, where residents can hold activities or meet with neighbours. In the existing towns and estates, such community spaces are added to the landscape through the Remaking Our Heartland (ROH) programme.

SMART & SUSTAINABLE

By tapping on smart urban solutions and innovative technologies, HDB seeks to develop towns that are liveable, efficient, sustainable, and safe. To guide the implementation of smart initiatives, HDB developed a Smart HDB Town Framework, which includes applications and services in five areas: Smart Planning, Smart Estate, Smart Environment, Smart Living, and Smart Community.

HERITAGE

In the planning and development of new towns and estates, HDB draws on their heritage and history to create distinctive identities and a sense of place. Some key terrain features could be retained while historical features like parks could be re-created. Some memorable landmarks could be kept, or markers and storyboards introduced to showcase the memories of the place. Themed playgrounds that reflect the history and heritage of an area have also been introduced in some places.

2 SMART AND SUSTAINABLE TOWNS

As the country's largest housing developer, HDB aims to build sustainable towns and play its part as a responsible developer.

HDB used to solely rely on 'passive design principles' that improve ventilation and minimise the reliance on air-conditioning by orientating blocks predominantly in the North-South direction. This reduced the amount of direct sunlight entering the flats and the subsequent build-up of heat.

The laundry drying system was placed at the periphery so that wet clothes could be dried naturally by the sun or wind, and blocks were designed with a secondary roofing system to mitigate heat gain for the topmost units.

But such practices have been updated with new technology.

HDB now uses data and computers to simulate wind flow and shadows cast by neighbouring buildings, to decide how blocks should be orientated in order to improve ventilation and lower the ambient temperature. It also uses solar energy to power precincts.

These new practices have been consolidated into several frameworks, including the Sustainable Development (SD) Framework in 2011 and the Smart HDB Town Framework in 2014.

The SD Framework is a holistic plan that sets out 10 desired outcomes for environmental, economic, and social sustainability.

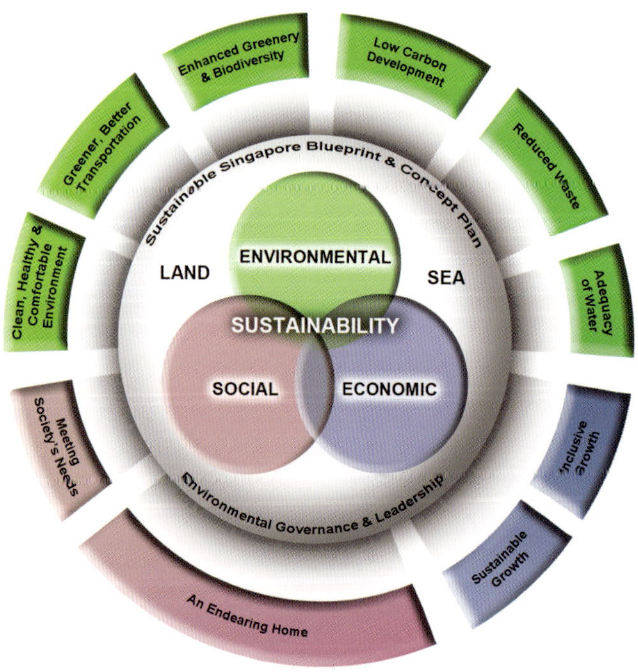

Sustainable Development Framework

ENVIRONMENTAL SUSTAINABILITY:

Reduce carbon emissions, optimise the use of resources, and achieve effective energy, water, and waste management.

ECONOMIC SUSTAINABILITY:

Generate economic vibrancy and business diversity in towns through innovative commercial facilities.

SOCIAL SUSTAINABILITY:

Encourage greater inclusiveness and social integration.

Punggol Eco-Town is the first HDB town developed under the SD Framework.

Under the framework, the town has adopted several initiatives such as the addition of extensive greenery to reduce the temperature of surrounding air, solar panels to generate renewable energy, LED lighting to save energy, and centralised chutes for recyclables to boost recycling rates.

The Smart HDB Town Framework maps out how information and technology can be used to develop smarter HDB towns – making them more liveable, efficient, sustainable, and safe.

Due to the sheer volume of flats that HDB constructs each year, these frameworks are coupled with construction technology to ensure that quality flats are built productively and safely.

Take prefabrication technology as an example. More than three in 10 new HDB projects use the Prefabricated Prefinished Volumetric Construction (PPVC) method, where three-dimensional prefabricated modular units with finishes are constructed and assembled in a factory setting before they are transported to the construction site for installation.

The technology cuts down the need for workers to work on the finishes at the construction site, reduces on-site manpower demands, and improves safety at worksites.

Cycling by the waterfront housing in Punggol.

Innovations from the beginning

'ARTIFICIAL Intelligence' and **'Big Data'** are among the biggest buzzwords, with new technology disrupting established industries. But at HDB, innovation is not new.

Veteran architect Dr Liu Thai Ker, who was the Chief Executive Officer from 1979 to 1989, said in an oral history interview in 1996 that public housing is **"as much a science as it is an art".**

In the 1970s, HDB studied the prevailing wind and sun angles to determine the best orientation for blocks. It also deliberated how it could minimise stuffiness inside flats by ensuring that the external walls did not absorb and retain too much heat.

By the 1980s, HDB had adopted prefabrication technology, where building components are manufactured off-site, then delivered and assembled on-site. This allows for better quality control.

Today, for every residential project, precast components make up about 70 percent of the total volume of structural concrete used in the construction stage. This saves man-hours and costs, improves the quality of finishes, and results in a lower dependency on manual labour.

In 2017, HDB inked a research and development agreement with the Nanyang Technological University (NTU) to develop a Smart Integrated Construction System (SICS).

The system will harness smart technology, through the use of smart sensors and automation, to transform traditional construction work processes. It will facilitate real-time data sharing and synergise construction processes across industry partners through a central digital platform to boost productivity and efficiency.

Smart Integrated Construction System

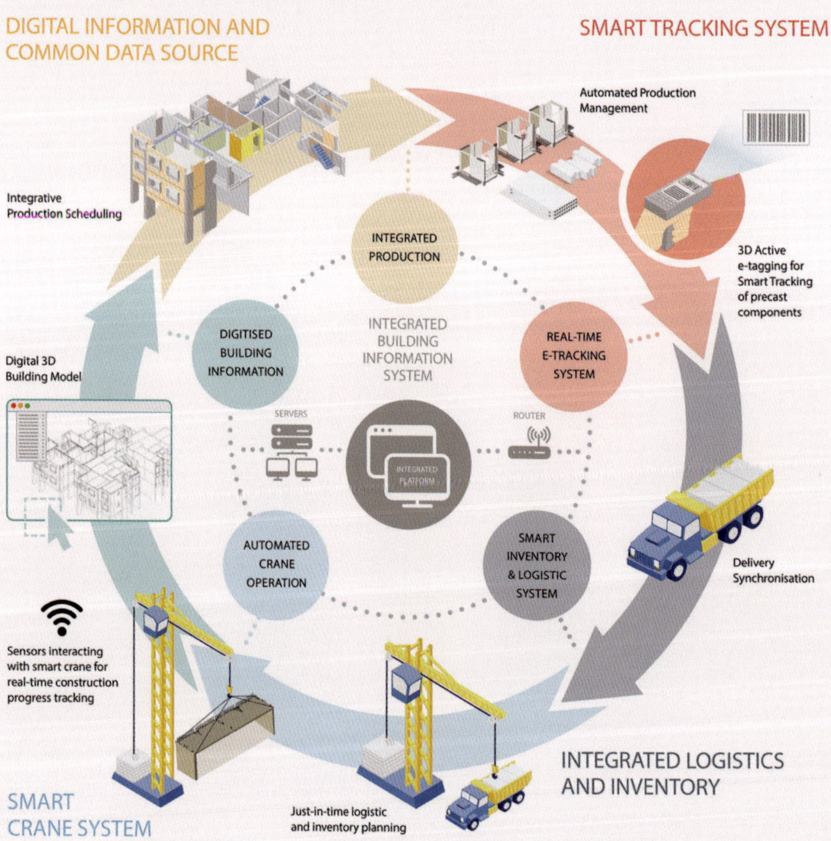

The science behind sunshine

Solar photovoltaic systems installed at the rooftops of HDB flats in Jurong West.

IN resource-scarce Singapore, there are a few forms of renewable energy available. The most promising and available option is solar energy.

For some years now, HDB has been exploring solar power as a form of green energy. Through the SolarNova programme, HDB aims to commit 70 percent of HDB blocks for solar panel installation by 2030.

At the start, HDB funded, procured, and installed solar photovoltaic (PV) systems on the rooftops of HDB blocks. It subsequently adopted a leasing model where the private sector funds, installs, operates, and maintains the solar PV systems.

The public-private partnership facilitated the rapid scale-up of solar energy usage in Singapore, as HDB continues to develop the science and collect data to monitor the solar panels' performance.

The data, in turn, is used to optimise the solar panels and help them work more efficiently and effectively.

"It is not always easy for organisations to go green," said CEO Dr Cheong Koon Hean. **"But because we were prepared to take risks and trial new technology, new ideas on design, and new ways of building, we were able to do it."**

When technology redefined how rubbish was collected

ONE of the first questions CEO Dr Cheong Koon Hean had when she joined HDB was why blocks were always constructed with driveways surrounding them.

Was it possible to have fewer driveways, in order to create a safer environment and introduce more greenery instead?

The driveways served a specific purpose. The refuse collection system in older HDB estates requires waste to be collected manually from multiple refuse chambers located around the blocks, and consolidated at a bin centre within the estate where it is picked up by a refuse truck. In newer estates where waste is deposited into centralised chutes, it would be picked up directly from the centralised refuse chamber beneath every block. Driveways are thus needed for rubbish trucks to reach the bin centres or centralised refuse chambers.

In response to Dr Cheong's question, HDB began to look for new technology that could solve the issue. It found its answer in the Pneumatic Waste Conveyance System (PWCS).

The automated waste collection system uses vacuum suction technology to transport household waste from each refuse chute to a centralised bin centre via a network of underground pipes. Instead of moving from block to block, a rubbish truck now only needs to collect rubbish from the one centralised bin centre serving some 2,500 to 3,000 flats.

The new technology requires less manpower to collect waste. It has also redefined how new HDB developments are designed. **"In some of our new projects, we can do away with the driveways for the rubbish trucks. Instead, we can now do more landscaping, creating a more walkable and safer environment for our residents,"** shared Dr Cheong.

This diagram illustrates how the Pneumatic Waste Conveyance System transports household waste from each refuse chute to a centralised bin centre via a network of underground pipes.

WHEN OLD BECOMES NEW AGAIN

HDB is also concerned about another facet of sustainability – ensuring that older towns and estates remain pleasant for residents. In fact, estate renewal is one of the key emphases of public housing in Singapore.

Introduced in 1995, the Estate Renewal Strategy (ERS) is a comprehensive and coordinated approach to rejuvenate and refresh older HDB estates. It encompasses SERS, as well as upgrading programmes that cover every aspect of heartland living including the Main and Interim Upgrading Programmes, and the Lift Upgrading Programme (LUP). For example, lift services are upgraded under the LUP to provide lift access on every floor.

In August 2007, the Main Upgrading Programme was replaced by the Home Improvement Programme (HIP), where improvement works such as repairing spalling concrete and structural cracks are carried out.

The Neighbourhood Renewal Programme (NRP) also took the place of the Interim Upgrading Programme, focusing on block and precinct improvements. Enhancements such as covered linkways and drop-off porches are built, and new community facilities such as multi-generation playgrounds and community gardens added.

Selected older precincts with redevelopment potential are renewed under SERS, and ageing towns are comprehensively rejuvenated as part of the ROH programme.

TOP: The Lift Upgrading Programme provides lift access to every floor to bring greater convenience to more residents.

BOTTOM: Under the Home Improvement Programme, laundry poles holders are replaced by a studier rack.

REFRESHED AND RENEWED

Since the 1990s, HDB has rolled out multiple initiatives and programmes to upgrade older towns and flats.

DATA OF UPGRADING PROGRAMMES

	YEAR	NO. OF TOWNS/ ESTATES	NO. OF FLATS/SHOPS BENEFITTED
Remaking Our Heartland	from 2007	9	-

	YEAR	NO. OF PROJECTS	NO. OF FLATS/SHOPS BENEFITTED
Main Upgrading Programme	1990 to 2007	129	131,000
Interim Upgrading Programme	1993 to 2001	190	156,000
Lift Upgrading Programme	from 2001	434	500,000
Interim Upgrading Programme Plus	2002 to 2006	84	62,515
Barrier-free Estate Programme	2006 to 2012	-	7,800
Home Improvement Programme	from 2007	-	320,000
Neighbourhood Renewal Programme	from 2007	79	116,000

	YEAR	NO. OF BLOCKS	NO. OF FLATS/SHOPS BENEFITTED
Project LIFE	1993 to 2011	53	15,770
Rental Flat Upgrading Project	2001 to 2010	76	15,541
HDB Greenprint	from 2012	78	8,994
Revitalisation of Shops	from 2007	-	1,800
Selective En bloc Redevelopment Scheme	from 1995	387	40,623
Enhancement for Active Seniors Programme (Direct Application)	from 2012	-	77,260

The information is accurate as at December 2019.

3 COMMUNITY-CENTRIC TOWNS

Across all HDB towns, residents of different ethnic groups and citizenship status live, eat, and play together. This harmony was not achieved by accident, but by design, largely owing to the Ethnic Integration Policy (EIP) and the Singapore Permanent Resident (SPR) Quota.

The two policies cap the proportions of different races and non-Malaysian permanent residents within individual neighbourhoods and blocks. They work in tandem to maintain a balanced ethnic mix in all HDB estates, as well as to foster better integration.

Take a walk through the HDB towns and it becomes clear that the policies have worked, for each neighbourhood is a microcosm of Singapore's multicultural society. Residents of all races have built strong community ties, and accept and accommodate the varied practices and customs of each ethnic group.

At the same time, the spaces are carefully designed to facilitate interaction among residents.

Eateries in neighbourhoods offer diverse cuisines of different ethnic groups. There is chicken rice, *nasi padang* (a Malay cuisine where steamed rice is served with an assortment of side dishes), and *roti prata* (a South Indian flatbread usually served with mutton or fish curry) under one roof. Friends and neighbours of different races eating together at the same table is also a common sight.

In the design of its new-generation towns, HDB has increased the provision of social and communal places to encourage more interaction among residents. These include spacious plazas for large group activities in town centres and new neighbourhood centres, where residents can gather for their workout sessions and mass activities. Skyrise gardens, community living rooms, and precinct pavilions provide additional places for neighbours to sit together and chat.

Located within the vicinity of facilities, such as Heartbeat@Bedok and Bedok Mall, Bedok Town Centre is a hive of activity in the Eastern part of Singapore.

HDB has also expanded its programmes to encourage residents to initiate projects that bring the community together. The Lively Places Programme that HDB jointly administers with the Urban Redevelopment Authority (URA) supports and funds community-led efforts to enliven Singapore's public spaces.

This includes event initiatives, such as community art workshops or larger-scale events, where community plazas are transformed into active spaces with games, activities, and performances. The fund also supports projects that bring about a physical transformation of existing public spaces for community uses such as void deck makeovers and setting up of community gardens.

Former Minister for National Development Mr Lawrence Wong at the September 2018 launch of the LIVINGSPACE, a gallery at HDB Hub showcasing how HDB has evolved from building basic functional housing to creating well-designed, sustainable and smart, and community-centric homes. L-R: HDB Chairman Mr Bobby Chin, Mr Wong, and HDB CEO Dr Cheong Koon Hean with children at the Dragon Playground exhibit in the LIVINGSPACE.

To further enhance interaction and to be more inclusive, HDB began building blocks that integrated rental and sold units in 2014. The first four of such BTO projects are located in Woodlands, Bukit Batok, Sengkang, and Pasir Ris.

Beyond the EIP and SPR Quota, HDB also designs its policies and plans to emphasise community centricity.

In the last few years, HDB has made several tweaks to its policies. The changes ensure flats remain affordable and accessible, and that home ownership is an attainable goal. They also encourage families to live with or near each other for mutual care and support, with targeted measures that cater to the diverse needs of married couples, singles, seniors, and divorcees.

Some notable adjustments to policies include a move in 2011 to stabilise prices of new BTO flats, by increasing the government subsidy to ensure that new flats remained affordable to first-timer households, and that BTO prices do not follow the same extent of resale price changes.

Mr Lawrence Wong, former Minister for National Development, elaborated on the reasons in a 2018 speech in Parliament: **"We cannot just leave things to chance… we must deliberately plan for a more equal and inclusive society… This means that families grow up in the same neighbourhood, and the residents share the same common areas and facilities."**

THE DECADE OF CHANGE

HDB has made significant strides in the last decade. It has successfully delivered the ambitious goal it had set back in 2010 when there was a lack of supply, and cleared the demand backlog within a few years.

At the same time, it drew up refreshed plans for public housing and put them into practice in new residential towns, estates, and precincts. The key to its success was to have a keen understanding of its customers, and a commitment to put them at the centre of every plan and policy.

To deliver good homes and towns, HDB has to understand the people it is building for – their lifestyles, aspirations, and demands.

After all, a home is not just a single unit in an HDB block. It is a holistic living experience, complemented by housing policies and schemes that help different groups of people at different stages of their lives meet their needs and aspirations.

> "We may be a housing developer with engineers and architects. But we are not just in the housing business – we are really in the people business."
>
> **Dr Cheong Koon Hean**
> Chief Executive Officer

Tampines GreenRidges

In a people business, service is key

BUYING a flat is one of the biggest financial commitments for most residents.

The process is also emotive. A home is not just four walls and a roof. It is a personal sanctuary for solace and strength.

Recognising this, HDB developed the HDB Service Master Plan in 2011 to deliver a more positive and seamless customer experience. The key shift was to move from a transaction-centric approach to a customer-centric one.

This journey starts at the beginning, when HDB customers begin sourcing for a flat, and lasts right till they move into their new home.

More than 200 electronic services are accessible via the HDB InfoWeb and the Mobile@HDB app, built with a Mobile Concierge feature, that work to simplify processes for customers.

Currently, about 99 percent of HDB transactions are done via these e-platforms that provide round-the-clock service.

But the human touch still matters.

The HDB Hub in Toa Payoh was given a facelift in 2016, with the first storey revamped to enhance customers' service experience. A video analytics solution helps HDB study crowd patterns, so that it can better plan manpower to cope with higher volumes of customers. HDB Service Ambassadors are also around to look out for customers who need more help.

FLAT APPLICATION

Customers can apply for a flat anywhere, anytime during the sales launch through HDB's digital platforms, and use its chatbot, Ask Jamie, for enquiries.

FLAT SELECTION

Every flat buyer has an individualised My HDBPage account with a progress tracker to update them on the status of their transactions, correspondence, and flat construction. Flat buyers will receive an email and SMS informing them of their flat selection appointment and the documents to bring. They will also receive an SMS reminder three days before the appointment.

MYNICEHOME ROADSHOW

The MyNiceHome Roadshow, which opens up opportunities for flat buyers to forge ties with their future neighbours and learn more about their living environment, is held three to six months before the completion of the first block for each BTO project. Flat buyers can also pick up useful home renovation tips and advice on home maintenance.

KEYS COLLECTION

When their flat is ready, customers will receive an email and SMS informing them to collect their keys. They can then book an appointment with HDB at their convenience via the online e-Appointment service.

MOVING-IN

Customers can easily arrange for home inspections through HDB's Virtual Building Service Centre (BSC) if they have feedback on their new homes, instead of having to go down personally to the centre.

LIVING-IN

HDB provides a hassle-free experience if its customers need any housing management services. They can easily tap on HDB's end-to-end e-services over its digital platforms, or book an appointment with an HDB officer online to schedule a more in-depth discussion.

SELLING OR BUYING A RESALE FLAT

Customers who wish to sell their existing flat or buy a resale flat can do so via the HDB Resale Portal launched in 2018. Through the portal, they can complete their transaction within eight weeks, and only need to come to HDB for one appointment. Previously, the wait was 16 weeks with two in-person appointments. By leveraging technology and data, the valuation process for buyers who use their CPF savings or take a housing loan for the flat purchase has also been streamlined, resulting in about 50 percent savings in time and cost. With these initiatives, the total number of citizen-hours saved from January 2018 to June 2019 amounted to about 310,000 man-months.

"Even as HDB taps on technology to provide more convenience for customers, the human touch remains essential, especially at the significant moments of life of our residents, such as the collection of keys to their new flats," shared Mr Randy Lim, Assistant Chief Executive Officer (Corporate).

"Digitalisation has thus transformed the way we work, so that our resources can be channelled to perform more personalised face-to-face engagement."

This includes financial counselling for residents who are unable to meet their mortgage instalment payments, reaching out to residents about programmes such as the Lease Buyback Scheme (LBS) and HIP, and advocating home ownership to rental tenants.

Mr Randy Lim, Assistant Chief Executive Officer (Corporate)

Mr Derek Tan, Group Director (Housing Management)

YEAR	VOLUME OF COUNTER TRANSACTIONS
2011	2,619,594
2019	602,451

Mr Derek Tan, Group Director (Housing Management) added: **"There is a common misperception that the introduction of e-platforms will replace all face-to-face services, and this will compromise service delivery or disadvantage customers who might not be as digitally-savvy.**

"This will not be the case for HDB, as our approach is to channel-match – adopting the platform best suited for the nature of transaction and customer profile."

Evolution of HDB's service delivery

1995

HDB launches its HDB InfoWEB to provide information to customers round the clock.

1997

HDB allows online submission of resale application and valuation requests by listed housing agencies.

1999

HDB launches more interactive content and e-services to facilitate communication with customers.

2000

HDB launches its electronic flat application system, allowing the public to submit online applications to buy flats.

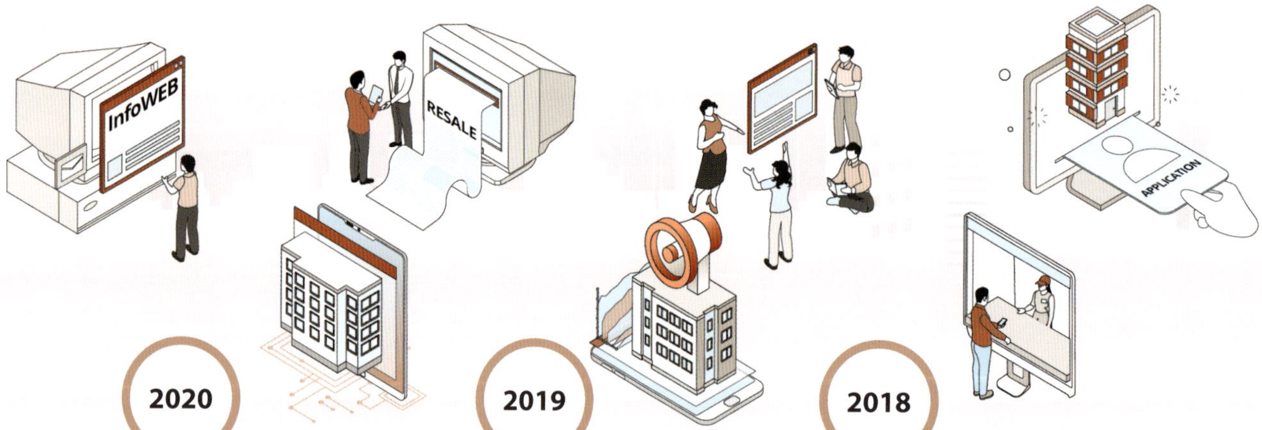

2018

HDB launches the HDB Resale Portal, which halves the transaction time from 16 to eight weeks as well as the number of appointments from two to one.

HDB implements its Service 3.0 Project, looking into processes affecting residents such as the HIP.

2019

HDB unveils plans for a new portal, which will allow sellers to list and advertise flats online, and process the resale application on the same platform.

2020

HDB increases its digital focus on service delivery, as it ramps up efforts to enhance the digital service experience for customers with its digital-first service strategy.

2006

HDB introduces personalised information and e-services through My HDBPage.

2011

HDB develops the HDB Service Master Plan to move from a transaction and operations-centric approach to a customer-centric one. Three strategies formed this Master Plan: balancing a personal customer experience with digital e-services; strengthening capabilities in service delivery and deploying new technology; and continuously engaging with customers and stakeholders.

2013

HDB adopts a value-chain approach to evaluate its customer experience by drawing up customer journey maps to identify and improve customers' needs.

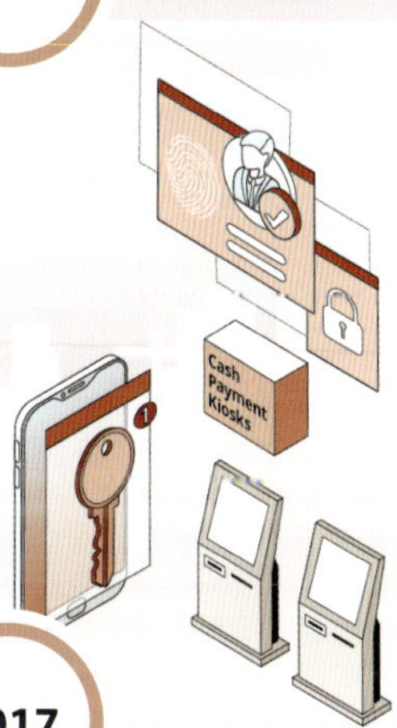

2017

HDB establishes an online key collection appointment system, which enables most flat buyers to book their key collection date. This helps HDB optimise its manpower resources.

HDB implements self-help Cash Payment Kiosks with end-to-end solutions at all HDB Branches in an effort to achieve zero payment transactions over the counter.

HDB introduces the HDB Experience Programme to align all HDB staff to the HDB service vision, equipping them to deliver better in-person interactions with customers.

2016

With the 3E (Enhancing Engagement Efforts) Project, HDB begins reviewing engagement strategies to create a seamless experience for residents in their flat-buying journey and improve its engagement efforts. For instance, HDB now reaches out to new home buyers about three to six months before the completion of their precinct through MyNiceHome Roadshow, to provide information regarding preparations for their new homes.

As new residents may approach their Grassroots Advisers on flat matters, HDB also invites the Advisers to preview the flats so as to give greater assurance of the quality of the new flats.

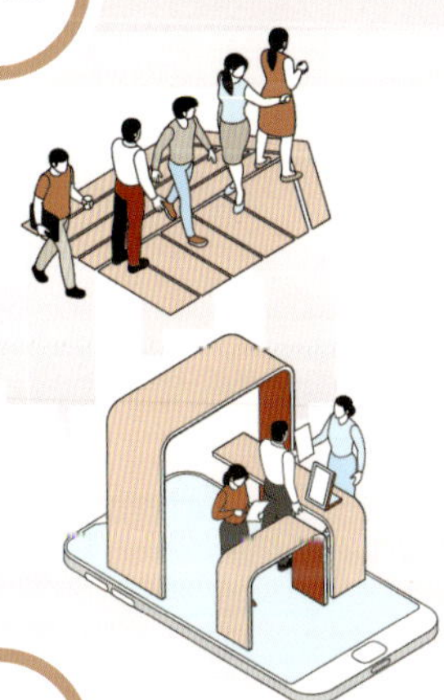

2015

HDB completes the suite of electronic services for high-volume Season Parking transactions and successfully digitalised more than 90 percent of counter transactions.

In the CEO's words...

Dr Cheong Koon Hean
Chief Executive Officer

Could you describe the challenge you had to confront at HDB when you joined the organisation in August 2010?

WHEN I joined HDB, the immediate big task was to ramp up our construction programme to deliver more flats to people. But I also saw it as an opportunity to build a whole new generation of public housing. Our public housing has been great, but lifestyles and aspirations have changed. And we have to keep up with the times too.

What would you say is the key strength of HDB?

The strength of HDB is that it is both the master planner and the master developer. HDB can provide a creative overall vision for the town and develop it comprehensively over the years to realise the vision. It lays out the land uses and transport network and the urban design guidelines that will shape the town. Residents benefit not only from having housing, but are well-served by a range of commercial, social, and recreational amenities.

The successful development of Punggol as a sustainable waterfront town is a prime example. HDB conceptualised it as a waterfront eco-town. Today, Punggol is a model town with many sustainable and smart features. Through creative urban design, we have guided architects with our urban design guidelines to develop seven beautiful waterfront districts.

How has the Roadmap reshaped public housing?

The Roadmap has steered HDB to deliver more exciting towns – the science is stronger and the quality is better. We strove to improve our service delivery too. At the same time, we reviewed many of our policies to ensure that housing continues to be affordable and meet the needs of different segments of the population.

How would you sum up the last 10 years at HDB?

With the Roadmap as a guide, we developed the technology and the research to create better designs and to build towns with improved functionality. Through innovative design, we do not just provide the four walls of your flat, but a total living environment that is attractive and pleasant, and will encourage greater community interaction.

To me, the last decade has been about managing change – to be more forward-looking and to take a bit more risk. It is about getting HDB to be more future-ready. We have built up more competencies, and we must continue to improve. But I would say I have a great team of colleagues who are prepared and excited to try new things.

CHAPTER 2

DESIGNING HOMES
FOR BETTER LIVING

" As Singapore becomes denser, we have to ensure that our towns are liveable by planning and designing innovatively, while still providing for a complete live, work, learn, and play environment, thereby catering to the different needs of the residents. "

Mr Fong Chun Wah
Deputy Chief Executive Officer (Building)

What do a former military training ground, an old cemetery, and a grass patch about the size of a football field have in common?

Disparate as they sound, all three parcels of land have transformed into distinctive public housing developments at different scales of infrastructure and detail – Tengah, an 'evergreen forest' town; Bidadari, a residential estate inspired by heritage and infused with nature; and Kampung Admiralty, a novel integrated complex.

Well-designed towns form one of the three key thrusts in the Housing and Development Board's (HDB) Roadmap to Better Living in HDB Towns. This ensures public housing is both aesthetically pleasing and functional. Beyond town planning, design also plays a crucial role in shaping homes.

Each HDB flat is shaped by architectural design that accommodates different family units. For instance, 2-room Flexi flats have become a viable option for many seniors, singles, and small families, while roomy Three-Generation (3Gen) flats are popping up in many towns to cater to generations of families wanting to live under the same roof. Good design allows us to carve out more space in our compact city, giving residents more greenery or open space.

With the aim of transforming Singapore's limited land into boundless living possibilities, planning and designing for towns, neighbourhoods, and homes in HDB towns is an intensive and intricate process.

HOW TOWN PLANNING EVOLVED

IN the early years of high-rise living in Singapore, designing a new town was straightforward. The urgency to solve the housing shortage then meant massive slab blocks were rapidly erected and replicated across different parts of the island. From Toa Payoh to Ang Mo Kio, the towns took on a similar look.

But as Singapore became increasingly affluent, social aspirations and expectations for public housing grew. Town planning and development began to focus on urban form, new town structures, and the provision of facilities such as regional parks and shopping malls.

Inspired by Southeast Asia's terraced rice fields, Waterway Terraces in Punggol stands out for its cascading blocks.

Towns became more visually distinctive through the use of different building typologies, form, materials, and even colours. Blocks at Potong Pasir became known for their sloping roof forms, while pitched roofs defined the flats at Bishan.

Under the Design and Build Scheme, HDB invited private architectural firms to conceptualise and construct flats. This gave rise to more interesting building typologies and form such as the first Design and Build project at Tampines Street 45 / Tampines Avenue 7. Its hexagonal layout design and red brick façade made it an iconic project in Tampines. Other buildings with interesting typologies include the cascading blocks of Waterway Terraces in Punggol, and the sky gardens at The Pinnacle@Duxton and SkyTerrace @ Dawson.

The designs of the 24 HDB towns and three estates that house over 80 percent of Singapore's resident population today have evolved immensely.

There has since been greater emphasis on creating a quality living environment built on precincts, neighbourhoods, and towns that are imbued with distinct identities, as HDB continues to push the boundaries of housing concepts. Urban design has also become a key focal point.

The 'checkerboard pattern' juxtaposes high-rise developments and low-rise amenities to create an interesting and varied skyline.

While architectural design only focuses on the look and function of individual buildings, urban design looks at shaping whole neighbourhoods and public spaces. It guides how developments in HDB towns relate to the surrounding environment – manifested in the many precinct gardens and common greens that weave through residential developments, or how buildings are purposefully designed and heights varied to avoid having a wall-like effect on the streets. Such an approach offers a third dimension to towns, enhancing the liveability of each neighbourhood.

In formulating land use plans, high-rise and high-density developments are interspersed with low-rise amenities, such as parks and schools, to provide spatial and visual relief. Called the 'checkerboard pattern', it offers residents a more interesting and varied skyline.

"As the master planner and master developer, our interest is in building a beautiful town that fits in with everything – all your commercial and social activities. The challenge is to be able to relieve the high density with interesting forms and a juxtaposition of building heights, public spaces, greenery, and water bodies," explained Chief Executive Officer, Dr Cheong Koon Hean.

CREATING DISTINCT IDENTITIES WITH DESIGN GUIDES

HDB conceptualises the vision for each town based on the distinct character and features that reflect the town's history. It also formulates the overall master plan and urban design guidelines, and develops the town hand in hand with various agencies. To ensure that all towns are built and upgraded according to the original vision and master plan, HDB developed Town Design Guides. The first Town Design Guide for Woodlands was published in 2018, followed by the Pasir Ris and Tengah Town Design Guides in 2020, with more guides to be rolled out progressively.

These guides are shared with all developers, public agencies, Town Councils, and designers, so that everyone has the same design reference. They will help to maintain a sense of design coherence and aesthetic quality of the town as it undergoes further development and upgrading over time.

"HDB takes great effort in formulating the vision and concept for every HDB town. The HDB town takes many years to evolve and many players play a role in realising the vision. The town will also undergo upgrading as the years go by," said Dr Chong Fook Loong, Group Director (Research & Planning).

"It is important that every designer, consultant, contractor, and Town Council that carries out work within the town understands the original concept and intent of the town master plan. This will ensure that the original vision and urban design intent for the town remain intact and are not diluted over time."

For example, when HDB carries out upgrading works, it may implement linkways in projects. Having a Town Design Guide informs HDB's consultants on the form, colour palette, and material they can use to align with the overall urban design strategy of the town.

The Town Design Guide maps out planning and design intents using three key scales:

TOWN:
Provides the overarching vision through layers such as history to understand the evolution of the town, give context to the planning principles, and identify key corridors.

NEIGHBOURHOOD/DISTRICT:
Focuses on themes and concepts for areas at the neighbourhood or district scale that guide aspects such as public spaces, streetscape, colour palettes, and landscaping.

PRECINCT:
Outlines the details of individual projects such as precinct facilities, playgrounds, covered linkways, and street furniture and signages.

USING DATA TO POWER BETTER DESIGN

While design is a form of art, there is also a science to developing a town. Before planners hit the drawing board, HDB goes through an intensive process of analysing data and research findings to have greater clarity on the existing conditions of the area.

One way HDB collects data is by gathering feedback regularly from the public. Another is through social research studies.

The studies provide HDB with valuable insight on how to improve the town planning process. For example, by gathering residents' feedback on the distinctive town features they identify with, HDB can then establish unique themes for each town.

Getting a sense of the ground

THE HDB living experience is a big part of the Singapore story. To better understand the changing needs of the various stakeholders, HDB regularly conducts research studies and surveys.

One key study is the Sample Household Survey (SHS). First launched in 1968, the SHS is a large-scale study conducted once every five years, amassing a wealth of information ranging from demographic data to residents' satisfaction levels with housing.

In the 1960s and 1970s, when high-rise blocks first made their appearance in the cityscape, the surveys assessed residents' reception to high-rise living. Fast forward to the 2000s and beyond, the emphasis has shifted to community and liveability issues.

The most recent SHS in 2018 gave residents an opportunity to share their satisfaction levels with HDB living. Questions ranged from the design of their flats to the strength of community ties in the heartlands. It also explored new topics like online shopping and surveyed residents about unique places in their towns that hold special memories for them. The responses have helped HDB better design meaningful communal spaces, and formulate new strategies to deepen the residents' sense of belonging to their towns.

HDB also conducts post-occupancy reviews after residents move in, as well as evaluative studies to gather residents' feedback on new initiatives and programmes. Such feedback informs HDB about residents' preferences and their receptiveness to new initiatives, enabling it to continuously refine housing designs.

The data will help shape the planning of future residential towns to keep up with the evolving lifestyles and preferences of residents.

The focus of the Sample Household Survey evolved over the decades, in tandem with residents' changing needs.

TENGAH: FOREST TOWN OF THE WEST

LOCATED in the Western region of Singapore, Tengah is expected to provide 42,000 residences when fully developed. Alongside other developments, including the Jurong Lake District, a mixed-use business district, and the advanced manufacturing campus of the Jurong Innovation District, HDB's 24th town will provide new living, working, and recreational opportunities.

Tengah has a history rooted in agriculture, with fruit tree plantations, farms, and villages populating the area back in the 1950s.

This village vibe was replaced by an industrial identity when private brickworks were set up in the 1960s. In the 1980s, Tengah transformed again as villages were resettled, and the area became a military training ground.

Today, Tengah is coming full circle. Plantations, farms, *kampungs*, and brickwork will be making a comeback – with a modern twist.

A GREEN FOREST AT THE DOORSTEP

The sprawling 700 ha site – about the size of Bishan town – is set to lay claim to many firsts.

Tengah was conceptualised as an 'evergreen forest' town that will be invigorated by abundant greenery and nature. It will become the first HDB town in Singapore to be fully integrated with the surrounding natural environment.

In collaboration with the National Parks Board (NParks), a 5 km long and 100 m wide Forest Corridor will run through the town as part of a larger network of greenery connecting the Western Water Catchment Area and Central Catchment Nature Reserve.

The Forest Corridor will be complemented with a continuous stretch of lush greenery, serving as a Forest Fringe that wraps around the town within a scenic and natural landscape.

At the heart of Tengah lies a 20 ha Central Park, where a Forest Amphitheatre and water bodies will create a picturesque backdrop for recreational activities. These amenities will be located within the planned green corridors, and will be easily accessible via the Community Farmways.

These linear Farmways will traverse several housing districts within the town, encouraging residents to walk and cycle. The Farmways will also create opportunities for social interactions among the community through shared recreational activities, such as hobby farming and gardening.

In designing Tengah Town, HDB has managed to incorporate nature into Tengah's urban landscape, minimising the environmental impact and ensuring that Singapore's land use needs are met.

TOP: Artist's impression of the forest-like setting along the Forest Corridor.

BOTTOM LEFT: Artist's impression of the thematic playground and fitness stations along the Plantation Farmway. These activity nodes offer scenic and tranquil spots for residents to relax and enjoy various recreational activities.

BOTTOM: The Tengah Master Planning Team in front of the Tengah model at the HDB Atrium. L-R: Ms Chen Yanyi, Ms Cherie Yeo, Ms Wu Sau Ling, Mr Derek Chik, Group Director (Research & Planning) Dr Chong Fook Loong, Mr Joshua Ang, Mr Muhammad Ihsan Abdul Muthalib, Mr Willie Lum, Ms Li Chao Ying.

Achieving balance with nature

A sensitive approach was adopted during the planning of the town to integrate nature with the urban environment, so that residents can better connect with nature and enjoy its intrinsic benefits.

Prior to its development, HDB had engaged consultants to conduct an environmental baseline study on Tengah. This study provided important insights that were later incorporated into the detailed urban design of the town. For instance, it showed how housing developments could be woven into the natural environment while retaining as much of the existing topography as possible. Progressive clearing of the land was also key, as it provided ample time for the animals to find new habitats.

HDB, with the various agencies, continues to work closely with nature groups and wildlife consultants to achieve a balance between retaining natural areas and meeting development needs in Tengah.

Artist's impression of Tengah Town – Singapore's first smart and sustainable town, with green features and smart technologies.

Artist's impression of the green commuting that residents in Tengah can look forward to.

> Tengah is one of the new developments in the West, and we're excited to be living in a new town with innovations such as the car-free town centre, as well as living close to nature. It is something we're looking forward to.
>
> **Mr Dzulfiqar**
> A 27-year-old senior project manager and future Tengah resident

GETTING AROUND WITHOUT VEHICLES

Besides being a green residential hub, HDB's newest town will also attempt to establish a car-lite and people-friendly environment.

Tengah will be home to Singapore's first car-free town centre. At the Market Place, as it will be called, roads will run underground, freeing up spaces at the ground level for pedestrians and cyclists. With dedicated walking and cycling paths, residents can look forward to safe and seamless connections for green commuting throughout the town.

MAKING EASY CONNECTIONS

A comprehensive road and transport network in Tengah will ensure convenient travelling within and beyond the town.

Most bus stops will be within 300 m of residences, with bus services facilitating connections to nearby MRT stations and key destinations in the West, such as Jurong Lake District, Jurong Innovation District, and Nanyang Technological University (NTU).

Dedicated bus lanes will be planned in Tengah, providing a smoother riding experience for commuters. The town will also be served by the Jurong Region Line.

Tengah will eventually feature mobility corridors to provide for future transit networks and technology such as autonomous vehicles or self-driving vehicles.

COMING HOME

HDB has designed Tengah to be a town that mixes nature with the new development, as it pays homage to the fruit tree plantations, farms, and villages that once dotted the area in the 1950s.

The Plantation Farmway, part of the Community Farmways network, will be a throwback to the town's plantation history. About 2,000 sq m of space will be set aside for community gardening and farming in the Plantation District, encouraging residents to enjoy farm-to-table dining by growing their own produce and sharing their harvest at farmers' markets.

The 700 m long and 40 m wide Plantation Farmway will weave through the housing precincts, and connect the community and recreational facilities within the district.

Located within walking distance from homes, the Community Farmways will also feature thematic playgrounds, fitness stations, and other facilities that encourage play and exercise, serving as localised parks for residents to spend time with their family and neighbours. This will give them a sense of identity and place – that they have come home.

TENGAH IN NUMBERS

6 STELLAR IDEAS

THE vision for Tengah will be realised through six key ideas:

- **i. Creating an evergreen forest town**
- **ii. Creating five unique housing districts**
- **iii. Creating a smart and sustainable town**
- **iv. Enabling close-knit communities**
- **v. Providing networks for ease of movement**
- **vi. Providing paths for walking and cycling everywhere**

Artist's impression of Tengah Town.

5 UNIQUE HOUSING DISTRICTS

Greenery forms the main structure of Tengah. HDB has planned for five housing districts within Tengah, each with a distinct character: the Plantation, Park, Garden, Brickland, and Forest Hill Districts. Each of them will be designed to reflect the unique identity of the town.

i. Plantation District

The Plantation District was the first district to be developed. Under the theme of community farming, HDB has set aside ample space for gardening and harvesting produce.

II. Garden District

With the picturesque Tengah Pond and Central Park as its backdrop, the Garden District will showcase its identity through thematic gardens that engage the senses.

iii. Park District

As the hub and heart of Tengah, the Park District, located between the Forest Corridor and Central Park, will be home to a vibrant town centre.

iv. Brickland District

In keeping with the brick factories set up in the area during the 1960s, the housing blocks of the Brickland District will feature brick-like patterns and textures on accent walls and façade surfaces, and offer unobstructed views of the Forest Corridor.

v. Forest Hill District

Surrounded by the Forest Corridor and Central Park, the design of the Forest Hill District is based on the concept of 'living amidst nature'. Residents will be able to enjoy greenery and nature close to their homes.

Artist's impression of Tengah Town that is designed to be interspersed with green spaces, allowing residents to better connect with nature.

3 TRAITS

At home with nature:

Bordered by the Forest Corridor, the Central Park, and a Forest Fringe, Tengah will offer residents the chance to experience nature right at their doorstep. The linear Community Farmways will also provide dedicated spaces for residents to enjoy community gardening and urban farming.

Car-lite and moving around with ease:

Apart from the car-free town centre, all roads within Tengah will be lined with dedicated walking and cycling paths. The road networks can be configured to cater for future technologies such as autonomous vehicles or self-driving vehicles. Tengah will also be served by various transportation networks like the upcoming Jurong Region Line.

Smart and sustainable:

Tengah is the first HDB town to be planned with smart technologies applied town-wide from the outset, making it HDB's largest smart and sustainable development to date.

The town will feature initiatives such as smart lighting in common areas that will conserve energy, a dual bicycle rack system to encourage green commuting, and the smart Pneumatic Waste Conveyance System (PWCS) to promote a more hygienic and efficient method of waste collection and management.

BIDADARI: COMMUNITY IN A GARDEN

JUST a half-hour drive away from Tengah, a new estate is being built on land that used to be the site of rolling hills, picturesque ponds, and a peaceful graveyard: Bidadari.

Once home to the verdant Alkaff Gardens during colonial times, and later, Singapore's main Christian cemetery, and Muslim and Hindu burial grounds, this area off Upper Serangoon Road was forgotten and laid derelict after it was permanently closed for burials in 1972. Nature soon reclaimed the land, attracting birdwatchers and joggers seeking a park-like environment.

But the land did not remain fallow for long. There were exciting plans for the 93 ha site that is roughly the size of 150 football fields.

In 2013, then Minister for National Development Mr Khaw Boon Wan unveiled plans for Bidadari, a new estate which will comprise some 10,000 flats when completed.

Artist's impression of the aerial view of Bidadari estate.

FLOWING WITH NATURE

As with the development of Tengah, preserving Bidadari's natural features was HDB's first priority. After all, its gentle knolls and lush hills make up an extraordinary landscape that is not an everyday sight in Singapore's dense urbanscape.

Members of the HDB Bidadari Multi-disciplinary Master Plan team. L-R: Mr Tan Sze Tiong, Ms Shermin Ng, Ms Chloe Wan, Ms Wong Li Eng, Ms Tay Bee Choo, Ms Lim Shu Ying, Mr Lloyd Ng, Ms Leong Mei Lin, Mr Ricky Nagatie, Ms Jasmine Heng, Ms Phuah Hui Peng, Ms Ong Caiyi.

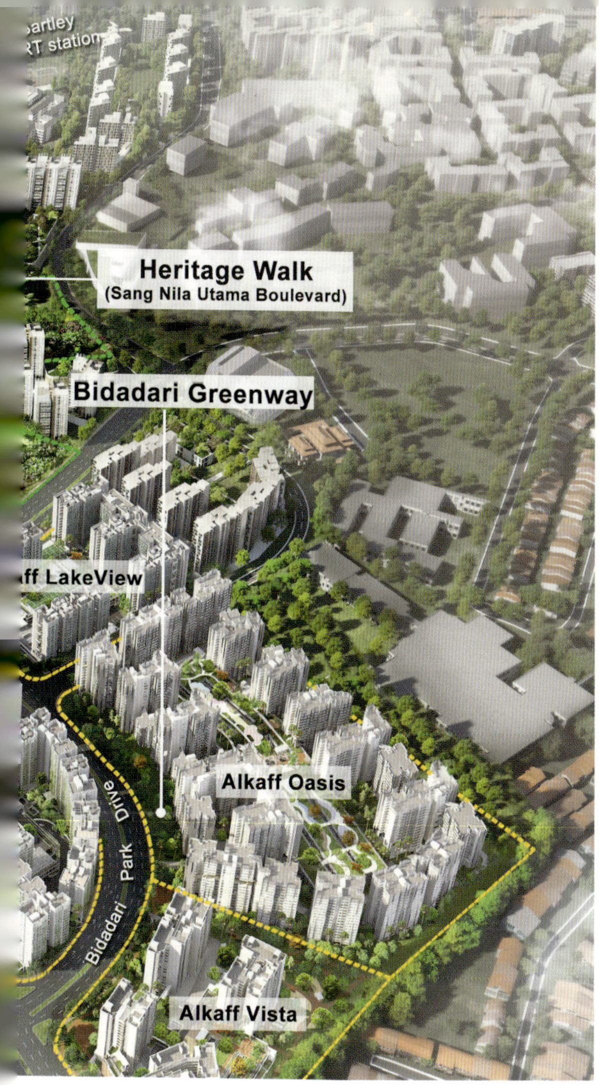

TOP: Artist's impression of the rooftop gardens at the multi-storey car park in Woodleigh Hillside.

BOTTOM: Architects and engineers from the Building & Research Institute's Centre of Design Excellence. L-R: Mr Eugene Leow, Mr Chia Yu Hsien, Mr Wan Khin Wai, Mr Sutomo Salim, Mr Wu Xianghua, Mr Leonard Cai, Mr Jonathan Chua (now with the Research & Planning Group), Mr Ng Peng Han, Mr Richmond Foo.

While flattening land is typically the quickest and easiest way to build infrastructure, HDB aimed to retain the natural terrain as much as possible.

To better understand what they were working with, the planning team conducted multiple site visits with NParks' arborists and nature groups over three years. They identified which trees to conserve during development, and camped in observation hides to bird-watch.

"We had to bash through the forest during different times of the day to observe the place, and got bitten by all sorts of insects," shared Ms Chloe Wan, Deputy Director (Urban Design Studio), with a laugh.

Armed with a clearer picture of the land that Bidadari was sitting on, the design team for Woodleigh Hillside was then able to work with what nature provided and minimise disruption.

"The idea was not to simply go in with a bulldozer," emphasised Mr Wan Khin Wai, Director (Urban Design and Development). **"If you flatten everything, it just seems like another manufactured environment. We used greenery to provide structure around the housing estate, rather than allow the estate to impose on nature."**

Multi-storey car parks, for example, were tucked into the natural slopes of the land, and their rooftops covered by gardens. Using this approach, large masses of man-made infrastructure were seamlessly blended into the natural environment.

"If you take a satellite image, you'll see that the spaces between the blocks are basically green areas and gardens. That's how Bidadari has become a community in the garden," added Mr Wan.

In addition, by working closely with the local conservation group Nature Society Singapore (NSS) and NParks, existing bird habitats on Hillock Park have been identified and retained. The residential blocks were also carefully planned to facilitate the movement of migratory birds, with new habitat zones created to enhance biodiversity.

REVISITING HISTORY, REKINDLING MEMORIES

It is a little-known fact that Bidadari's past extends beyond simply being a resting place for the departed. This was why the planning team wanted to shed some light on the mystique that surrounded Bidadari, which incidentally means 'fairy' in Malay, and reflect its rich history and heritage.

By interviewing historians and poring through old archives dating back to the early 1900s, the team identified long-lost landmarks and features that once defined the area. One historical feature was the Alkaff Lake Gardens – a pre-war Japanese-style garden that was a popular dating site for young couples during its time. Bidadari also hosted Singapore's first Malay-medium secondary school, the now-defunct Sang Nila Utama Secondary School.

These old memories will be rekindled. A big feature of the 10 ha Bidadari Park – helmed by a multi-agency collaborative effort involving HDB, NParks, Singapore's national water agency PUB, and the National Heritage Board (NHB) – is the new Alkaff Lake, named after its predecessor.

An existing memorial garden that commemorates the heritage of the former Bidadari cemetery will be integrated within the new Bidadari Park, while relics and tombstones of notable Singaporeans, such as philanthropists Dr Lim Boon Keng and Dr Chen Su Lan of the 1900s, will be relocated there. These will offer residents a glimpse into the area's important history.

Bidadari's enduring heritage will create a unique identity for its residents.

BUILDING BENEATH THE SURFACE

To meet various development needs within a limited land area, one key strategy HDB has employed in recent years is to integrate infrastructure seamlessly with the landscape. For example, within Woodleigh Village, a large bus interchange was tucked into a slope to minimise its visual and noise impact, with a hawker centre and 330 flats located above it.

Bidadari Park will hold Singapore's first underground service reservoir, which will store drinking water to regulate supply to homes, beneath a community lawn. Locating such utilitarian features beneath green spaces, which can simultaneously be enjoyed by the public, optimises land use and enables HDB to combine functionality and aesthetics within a small space.

Through such innovative strategies, the HDB team is able to balance different requirements within the new Bidadari estate, such as the need to incorporate nature and heritage, along with demands for development.

TOP: Artist's impression of the New Alkaff Lake within Bidadari Park.

BOTTOM: Artist's impression of Woodleigh Village.

In hot demand

HOMES in this central location have been highly sought after. When HDB first launched Bidadari projects for sale in November 2015, it received an overwhelming response.

Mr Zach Goh, 30, and his fiancée Ms Rennette Yeo, 32, were among the lucky ones. Come 2022, they will move into their brand new 4-room flat in Woodleigh Glen – a project that was planned and designed entirely by HDB's in-house team of architects and engineers.

"We wanted a place in Bidadari because it is near enough to both our parents' places," said Mr Goh. He is eagerly anticipating the final look of the project, which will boast ample greenery, including three storeys of green community spaces and a 200 m long sky terrace.

"But one thing we're most looking forward to is the new Bidadari Park," he added, noting that the upcoming 10 ha regional park nearby will be warmly welcomed by nature lovers like himself.

"We can take our dog there for walks, and just soak in the greenery. It will be great to be so close to nature."

Woodleigh Glen was designed with features that complement the natural setting. The HDB team used environmental modelling software to conduct studies that determined the ideal locations for rain screens along common corridors, without them blocking natural light and surrounding views.

Blocks were also arranged for optimal shade from the sun, while some void decks were designed to be built higher by half a storey, allowing natural wind flows to cool the community spaces at lower floors.

The project clinched the Innovative Design Award at HDB's Design Awards in 2017.

Come 2022, Ms Rennette Yeo and Mr Zach Goh will move into their new Bidadari home.

Green, blue, and beautiful

Artist's impression of Bidadari Park with Alkaff Lake and the Heritage Walk, surrounded by residential developments.

BIDADARI comprises four distinctive districts – Alkaff, Woodleigh, Park Edge, and Bartley Heights – which are complemented by a Market Square near Woodleigh MRT station. Each district will incorporate new housing forms that respond to Bidadari's unique terrain and characteristics. For example, within the Alkaff District, the layout of the housing blocks is a combination of slab blocks at staggered heights, configured to create pockets of green courtyard spaces. The housing blocks of varying heights also lend a diverse and interesting skyline that fronts Upper Serangoon Road and Bidadari Park Drive.

The estate's projects will include a variety of green features from green courtyards to sky terraces and rooftop gardens.

Private developments and facilities will be seamlessly integrated. One example is the upcoming Woodleigh Mall / Woodleigh Residences, which incorporates a community club and a Neighbourhood Police Centre. A bridge from Woodleigh Residences will provide direct access to Bidadari Park. Together with Woodleigh Village located across the Heritage Walk to the North, these two mixed-use developments will form the vibrant Market Square.

At the same time, Bidadari will also look to revive much of its rich heritage, achieving a balance between history and modernity.

Alkaff Lake

Inspired by the former Alkaff Lake Gardens, which was a popular site in pre-war colonial Singapore, the new Alkaff Lake in Bidadari Park will be a means to revisit the old times when families frequented the park to picnic and boat.

On rainy days, the lake will also double up as a stormwater retention pond to slow down and reduce peak stormwater run-off into the public drainage system, reducing the risk of floods. Other stormwater management initiatives include the Active, Beautiful, Clean (ABC) Waters design features within Bidadari's housing developments, such as rain gardens and bio-retention systems. These features naturally cleanse the stormwater run-off before it is discharged into the public drainage system, improving the water quality in catchment and waterways.

Heritage Walk

Part of the former Upper Aljunied Road will be pedestrianised into a Heritage Walk with a lush boulevard of conserved mature rain trees. A series of storyboards will be installed along the trail to allow visitors to learn about the history and stories of Bidadari's rich past. A segment of it will be named the Sang Nila Utama Boulevard to mark the site of the school that once stood on those grounds.

KAMPUNG ADMIRALTY: THE ONE-STOP RESIDENTIAL HUB

Kampung Admiralty – A modern-day *kampung*.

DESIGN BLUEPRINT: A VERTICAL *KAMPUNG*

OVER in Northern Singapore, a new integrated complex has emerged as a living lab for multi-generational interaction and multifarious amenities. Officially opened in 2018, Kampung Admiralty is the first HDB project to integrate public housing with healthcare, childcare, and eldercare facilities.

The compact and vertical compound is a one-stop hub that encourages community bonding and active living through innovative design, communal spaces, and sustainable features. For residents, there is little need to venture out of Kampung Admiralty. Everything required is comfortably within reach. There are shops, food stalls, and even a medical centre located within the commercial side of the building. These are separated from the residential blocks to ensure privacy for flat owners.

"I always joke with my wife that we don't even need to buy a fridge. The supermarket is just below. If we want anything, we can just go down and buy it fresh," quipped Mr Heng Gee Choo, a resident of Kampung Admiralty since 2017. **"I tell my friends that I have over 10 fridges at home. They're all just downstairs."**

"Aside from all these conveniences, there are also many daily activities organised throughout the year. There is never a dull moment."

Such activities include Zumba classes at the community plaza on the first floor, and the likes of art and cooking workshops at the Active Ageing Hub (AAH). They are so popular that even non-residents pop by to participate. Kampung Admiralty has become an attraction in its own right, receiving more than one million visitors in 2019.

At Kampung Admiralty, activities are conducted at the community plaza to encourage residents to stay active.

SMALL SPACE, BIG IDEAS

The idea for Kampung Admiralty first arose when HDB was deciding how to best make use of a small parcel of prime land barely the size of a football field, located right next to Admiralty MRT station and a neighbourhood centre.

The site was originally planned to be exclusively for residential use. But with such an ideal location – a rarity in land-scarce Singapore – HDB had bigger ambitions in mind.

"We decided to develop it into an integrated complex, bringing in a medical centre and a hawker centre that were originally planned to be across the road," said Mr Yap Chin Beng, who was Deputy Chief Executive Officer (Estate & Corporate) and Senior Advisor (Estate & Corporate), before retiring in 2019.

HDB opted for an unconventional and bold approach to fit everything together perfectly within such small parameters.

Working with architectural firm WOHA, the solution was to employ a 'club sandwich' approach. As it was impossible to expand laterally, the only solution was to go vertical and stack the facilities. Certain installations, such as the hawker, medical, and childcare centres, had to be built on different floors – just like ingredients layered in a sandwich.

But the unorthodox approach had its own set of challenges. As these facilities were traditionally built on the ground floor, some stakeholders were reluctant to move up to higher floors. There were competing needs to locate all the facilities at the prime space on the ground floor.

Beyond the resistance, the bigger challenge was to get all seven government agencies, including the Ministry of Health (MOH), the Early Childhood Development Agency (ECDA), and the National Environment Agency (NEA), to compromise on their preferences and priorities.

With so many parties involved, it was crucial for these agencies to work together towards a common vision. **"We had to do a lot of persuasion and regularly remind everyone that the whole is greater than the sum of its parts. The architectural design by WOHA also helped alleviate the partners' worries,"** said Mr Yap.

For example, there were concerns that the hawker centre would have low visibility if it were located on a higher floor. This would affect the business of the stallholders. However, this issue was rectified by designing the second-floor hawker centre to be easily visible from the bustling People's Plaza below.

Even though the facilities are located on the higher floors, WOHA ensured that they were still designed to provide users with the feeling of being based on the ground floor. For instance, there is a children's playground and a seniors' exercise area catering to both young and old on the sixth storey. It was an ideal location for ECDA to base its childcare centre there.

Each time Mr Heng picks up his granddaughter from childcare, he would take the opportunity to use the exercise equipment there while keeping a watchful eye as his granddaughter plays in the children's area.

The provision of these facilities has given residents of Kampung Admiralty an impetus to remain active, noted Mrs Lee-Loy Kwee Wah, Executive Associate of the Development & Procurement Group. **"We don't want the seniors to hide in their homes and not know what's happening outside. We try to draw them out with these activities, so that they can live an active lifestyle."**

A DESIGN THAT NURTURES RELATIONSHIPS

The integrated set-up at Kampung Admiralty has not only enhanced neighbourly ties, but also fostered strong inter-generational bonds. The partnership between the AAH and My First Skool best reflects this.

For instance, AAH participants will regularly head outdoors with the students and teachers. They usually make their way to the playground and fitness corner just outside the centre for interaction and playtime.

The children have certainly provided some much-needed energy to the seniors, noted My First Skool's principal, Ms Poh Jia Yi. **"We can see how the seniors care for the young, and we hope that this bonding will help the children learn to be respectful and considerate towards seniors."**

Most importantly, Kampung Admiralty has refined the art of ageing for its residents.

There are three key components to ageing well: comfortable adjustments, continual learning, and community support, according to Ms Chai Chee Mei of NTUC Health, who takes charge of curating all activities at the AAH.

"Kampung Admiralty provides a wholesome and natural environment to enhance this approach of ageing well. The residents enjoy many convenient services and options to live life more colourfully," she said.

In his speech at the official opening of the complex in 2018, Prime Minister Lee Hsien Loong said: **"HDB had looked for new ideas to develop**

Cooking up a storm at the Active Ageing Hub.

new designs that would fit an elderly population; to build flats, common areas, neighbourhoods that promote strong social support and community bonding; and to let people in their silver years stay socially engaged, and live safely, healthily, and happily."

This has, in fact, been the experience of many residents in the modern-day *kampung*. Just six months after they moved in, the Hengs have established solid friendships with many of their neighbours. With his affable personality and nifty repairman skills, Mr Heng has earned a reputation in his precinct as the 'village chief' – the go-to man who can help with anything from fused bulbs to emergencies. Mrs Heng is part of a clique that goes out to catch old Cantonese movies together.

"Everyone here is all about the same age. It's easier to bond and get along. Everything is catered towards people of our age," Mr Heng said. **"Our home is truly the only one of its kind in Singapore."**

ALL IN ONE

In line with its Roadmap, HDB is shifting towards building integrated developments with an array of facilities to cater to diverse needs. This integration concept is being explored in more projects around Singapore, depending on the specific needs of the community.

The Yew Tee Integrated Development in Choa Chu Kang Town is another such project. Plans were announced in September 2019, with completion estimated to be in 2026.

"Facilities used to take up individual parcels of land, so we're always in search of a better paradigm or solution. Although Singapore has finite land space, there are infinite possibilities to use the land optimally," explained Dr Chong Fook Loong, Group Director (Research & Planning).

TOP: Children from My First Skool and a senior at the Active Ageing Hub enjoying one another's company.

BOTTOM: Developing green fingers together.

A perfect space for two

THE Hengs' 36 sq m studio apartment is a cosy set-up, with just the right amount of space for the elderly couple.

They had moved into their home in Kampung Admiralty after right-sizing from a 4-room flat in Marsiling when their daughter moved out, as it became increasingly difficult to maintain a larger flat. Cleaning was a massive chore. At their old home, Mrs Heng Gee Choo would take two to three hours to mop the entire flat.

"Now, it only takes 30 minutes to mop the floor here, and she does it twice a day," Mr Heng said with a laugh.

For Mr Heng and his wife, the emphasis on safety at Kampung Admiralty is another plus point. All 104 units are outfitted with elderly-friendly features, such as ramps at the entrance to the unit and toilet, and grab bars in the toilets. Flats also come with resilient vinyl strip flooring to reduce the risk of slipping.

Mr Heng Gee Choo (right) with his wife and granddaughter.

Mr Heng no longer has to worry about leaving his kettle on the stove for too long. Unlike the conventional gas hob, the current built-in induction hob in his kitchen is equipped with a timer that automatically switches off the stove if it detects that the heat has been running for too long.

Studio Apartments are designed to provide ample space for elderly couples living on their own.

The award-winning architecture

A bird's eye view of Kampung Admiralty's roof garden.

KAMPUNG Admiralty has won several accolades, including the World Building of the Year – one of the world's most prestigious architectural awards – at the 2018 World Architecture Festival.

The development also emerged top in two award categories at the Chicago-based Council on Tall Buildings and Urban Habitat Annual Awards Programme in 2019. The awards recognise projects that have made exceptional contributions to the advancement of the urban environment, achieved high levels of sustainability, and had an immense impact on people.

NEW LIFESTYLE, NEW LAYOUTS

WITH an eye on the big picture, HDB has designed new towns and estates with distinctive identities and functions. But equally important is how HDB has also adapted to meet the shifting demands of residents by coming up with a range of new designs and layouts for flats.

Designs have progressively evolved in four key areas over the past decade:

1 UNIVERSAL DESIGN

Since 2006, HDB has applied this concept from the precinct level down to individual units, designing age-friendly neighbourhoods that will cater to Singapore's ageing society.

These include barrier-free routes between blocks and facilities, lift buttons with Braille markings and contrasting colours for easy visibility, and wider corridors and doorways in each house to accommodate wheelchairs.

"As our population is ageing, how can we design an environment that encourages independence? Every flat must be designed with that long-term lifespan and changing needs in mind," noted Mr Jeremiah Lim, Deputy Director (Design Policy).

2 DESIGNING FOR DIVERSE NEEDS

With most of Singapore's resident population living in public housing, HDB has to design homes that cater to a spectrum of different needs – from young to old, singles to married couples.

Residents now get more flexibility when it comes to home configuration. Most newer flats, for instance, will come with open kitchens that are more in line with current tastes, as opposed to having partition walls previously.

The open kitchen concept was introduced to cater to evolving lifestyles and preferences.

Mr Cheong Kin Man, Director (Design Development), and Mr Jeremiah Lim, Deputy Director (Design Policy)

"We look to understand the needs of residents and the changing lifestyle trends. Then we see how we can make the space more multi-purpose," explained Mr Cheong Kin Man, Director (Design Development).

3 DESIGNING FOR THE COMMUNITY

Shared spaces, such as playgrounds and precinct pavilions, play a crucial role in building bonds among residents.

In recent years, Town and Community Plazas have also become a key feature of HDB towns. Since the first plaza was introduced in Bedok in 2016, these spaces have become a place for staging the likes of food, music, and sporting events.

4 ENHANCING GREENERY AND LANDSCAPE

Incorporating greenery into urban areas has both practical and aesthetic benefits. It reduces surface temperatures and beautifies the town.

"When you're surrounded by concrete built-up area, greenery lends a softer and more pleasant environment. It is also visually pleasing and helps the mental well-being of residents," said Mr Cheong.

Ultimately, every design has a common goal: To achieve the best living conditions for residents.

NEW GENERATION NEIGHBOURHOOD CENTRES

WHEN residents step out of their new-generation homes, they are able to easily access the New Generation Neighbourhood Centres – designed to be communal, convenient, and connected.

One example is Oasis Terraces, an architecturally-striking building that complements its scenic surroundings. It features cascading multi-coloured gardens, lush green shrubbery that line the concrete exteriors and interiors, and a rooftop community garden.

This seven-storey complex is HDB's first New Generation Neighbourhood Centre. It is designed to be beautiful and functional, with comprehensive amenities such as a 24-hour fitness centre, supermarket, food court, and community plaza.

Apart from Oasis Terraces, the other New Generation Neighbourhood Centres include Northshore Plaza in Punggol, Canberra Plaza in Sembawang, and Buangkok Square in Hougang.

Neighbourhood Centres have always been an integral part of HDB towns. Strategically situated near residential blocks, these complexes provide convenient eating and shopping options close to home.

But as lifestyles evolved over the years, the design of these commercial facilities required a relook. One key update was to integrate more facilities within the centres due to land limitations.

In 2013, HDB resumed its programme of building and wholly managing neighbourhood centres. Having ownership of the properties gives HDB better oversight and greater flexibility to adjust facilities easily according to residents' needs.

LEFT: Buangkok Square features a variety of shops, and food and beverage outlets to serve the needs of residents.

TOP: At Oasis Terraces, residents and visitors can satisfy their retail and lifestyle needs all under one roof, with a waterfront view.

This is part of HDB's aim to provide a holistic town for residents, shared Deputy Chief Executive Officer (Building), Mr Fong Chun Wah.

"We don't want people to travel very far to these amenities. Most people will be able to shop and eat within the town area – that is one of the key fundamentals of our planning," he said. **"These new neighbourhood centres also provide other amenities besides commercial facilities and spaces for community activities.**

"It is very important to remember that we're not just about building flats. We're planning a town for residents to provide a complete and comprehensive environment. We have to cater to the different needs of the residents – not just the home where they stay, but the environment where they live as well," explained Mr Fong.

Today, the centrepiece of all New Generation Neighbourhood Centres is a community plaza – a focal gathering and mingling point for residents. At these centres, where there are younger retailers serving younger families, up to four festive events are organised per year at the community plaza and event spaces.

Apart from the commercial and thematic events, priority is also given to grassroots organisations, government agencies, and other organisations to bring in community events.

Since the opening of Oasis Terraces in February 2019, more than 200 events and activities have been held at the mall. Similarly, Buangkok Square, which also opened in February 2019, has seen more than 50 events and activities. All these programmes have brought vibrancy to the neighbourhood centres.

Oasis Terraces: One-stop destination for Punggol residents

An oasis for Punggol residents.

WHEN Punggol Plaza was built in 2004, it was the last neighbourhood centre that HDB developed. HDB wanted to cede this space to private developers, as they had the expertise in building suburban commercial malls.

But residents ended up unhappy. The private developers were not keen to build in new towns until there was a critical mass of residents, leaving those who moved in earlier with a lack of amenities.

In February 2019, HDB brought back the development of neighbourhood centres for the first time in more than 10 years, opening Oasis Terraces in Punggol – a seven-storey mall next to Oasis LRT station.

The intent was to cater to the needs of Punggol residents, who wanted shops and facilities, family friendly dining options, and sports and recreational facilities.

Unlike private developers, HDB's priority rests not on maximising commercial returns but meeting the needs of residents, former Minister for National Development Mr Lawrence Wong said at the official opening of Oasis Terraces.

"We don't maximise every single plot ratio. We have many open spaces, public spaces for residents to gather and mingle, and to achieve our social objective of strengthening family bonds and facilitating community integration," he noted.

For shop tenant Ms Deepika Jindal, 36, Oasis Terraces is like a second home. She runs Green-on-Go, selling eco-friendly products such as stainless steel straws and lunchboxes.

"You see kids running around, everybody knows one another, and they are kind and helpful," said Ms Deepika, who lives in the precinct next to Oasis Terraces.

Taking a refreshed approach to reviving neighbourhood centres – now known as New Generation Neighbourhood Centres – has allowed HDB to build a place outside of home and work, where residents can socialise and forge a sense of community.

Mr Mike Chan, Deputy Chief Executive Officer (Estate), believes that taking care of the commercial offerings in neighbourhood centres is an important way of making sure that they remain as relevant places for residents – an integral part of HDB living. Hence, more engagement with the residents and the commercial tenants is important as the retail scene is constantly evolving.

"Residents are happy only when the amenities in their area are enough, and they are the ones that they want," he said.

The 4 Cs of designing neighbourhood centres

CONNECTIVITY

They must be well-connected to the residential areas, with direct links to public transport nodes.

CONVENIENCE

They offer a vast array of commercial facilities and services. Oasis Terraces has 92 retail and food and beverage outlets spread over seven storeys, 12 education and enrichment centres, and even a collection lobby with parcel lockers. It also has a polyclinic to serve the growing population in Punggol.

COMMUNITY

They are designed to be community-centric, with ample community spaces. The sprawling plazas are vital in fostering community bonds and facilitating interaction among residents.

CONSULTATION

Residents share their vision of the new centres. For Oasis Terraces, residents were involved in focus group discussions and surveys, indicating that they favoured shops and facilities to have later closing times.

Cycling trail in Punggol.

CHAPTER 3

SMART AND SUSTAINABLE

HOMES THAT STRETCH THE IMAGINATION

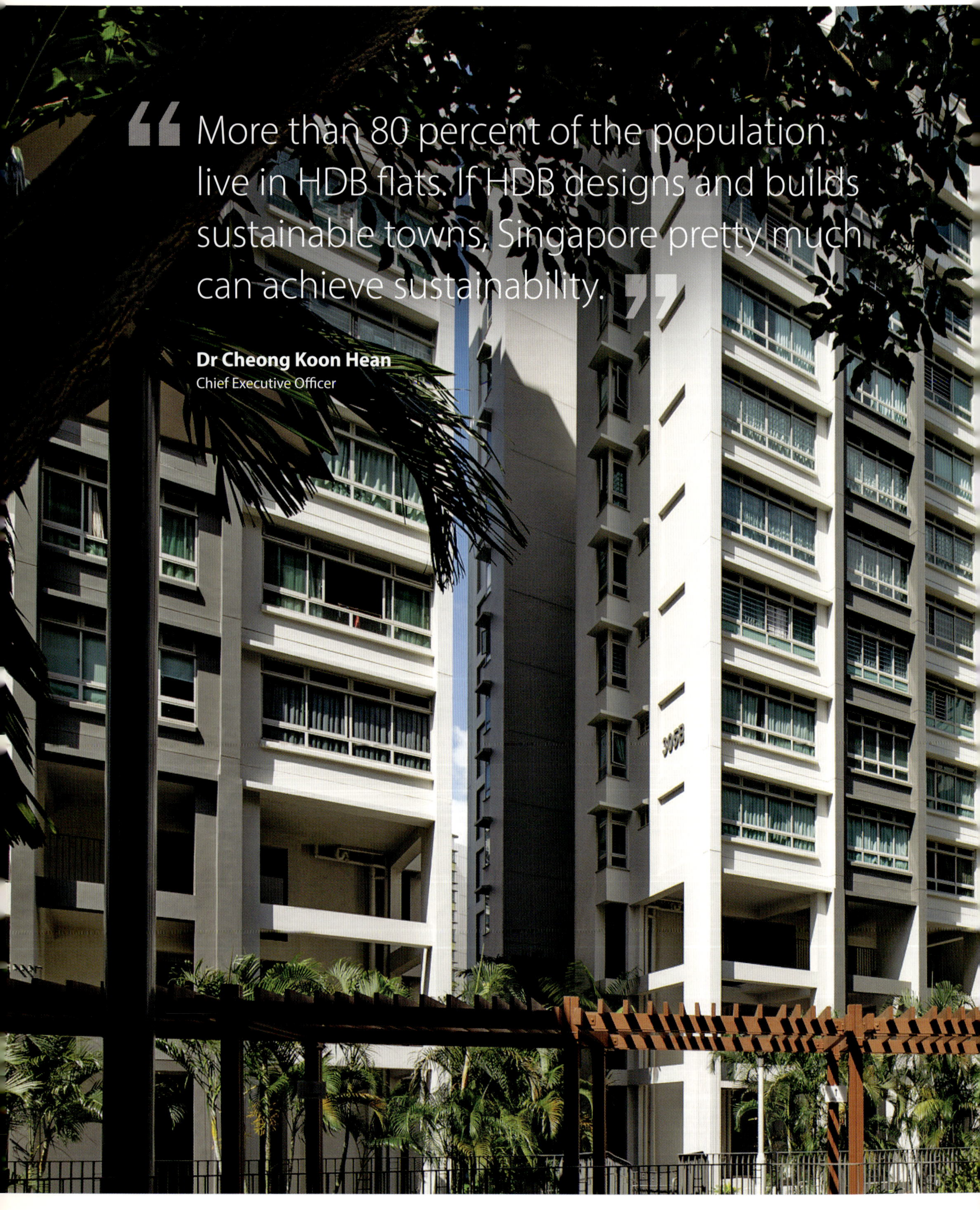

> More than 80 percent of the population live in HDB flats. If HDB designs and builds sustainable towns, Singapore pretty much can achieve sustainability.

Dr Cheong Koon Hean
Chief Executive Officer

A river created from scratch. An underground automated waste management system. And a data analytics centre with huge screens displaying real-time information on estate services in public housing island-wide.

These are not immediately nor intuitively associated with a public housing developer. But in Singapore, the Housing and Development Board (HDB) is entering unprecedented territory to offer residents homes that are smarter, greener, more efficient, and better maintained by going big on technology.

All of this is done for one key reason: Sustainability.

"Many cities aspire to be 'sustainable'. But to achieve true sustainability, we must have strategies backed up by science, and establish key performance indicators to measure success. Then we can keep improving further," shared Chief Executive Officer, Dr Cheong Koon Hean.

The resources were developed in-house, within a dedicated research institute that looks into engineering expertise and sophisticated urban planning and modelling software.

Frameworks were also set up to ensure that the initiatives are implemented in a cost-efficient and comprehensive manner. They consider economic and social sustainability too, with plans for towns to be self-sufficient in amenities and community spaces for social interaction.

These methods have found a testbed in coastal Punggol, which is blazing a trail for towns of the future.

One landmark project is the stunning waterway that meanders through Punggol. The other is Treelodge@Punggol – HDB's first eco-friendly precinct that uses passive design and green building technology for efficient energy, water, and waste management.

Treelodge@Punggol embraces Singapore's tropical climate. Solar panels power the services in the common area, while community gardening efforts beautify the area and build bonds among residents.

PUNGGOL: AN UPSTREAM JOURNEY ON THE WATERWAY

Prime Minister Lee Hsien Loong announced

Punggol 21 Plus

at the National Day Rally in 2007

WHERE do you start when you want to build a river? The sheer novelty of the challenge was one thing the HDB team grappled with.

"We studied plans for the Singapore River, the River Seine in France, and the River Thames in London to understand how rivers in an urban setting can be formed in a more natural way," recalled Dr Chong Fook Loong, Group Director (Research & Planning).

These local and foreign examples provided inspiration on how to align the waterway. The team even drilled down to the details of where to widen the river to minimise sedimentation.

Thought was also given to creating beaches like those by the River Seine. Drawing inspiration from the scenic French river, a sand playground was planned to be situated right by the waterway in Singapore's North-eastern town.

It was special and spectacular in design, as there was no other HDB town with a man-made water body running right through the middle like a Venetian canal, only greener and more natural.

Punggol's man-made waterway came to fruition after several re-drawings of the route.

The Adventure Bridge at Punggol Waterway Park offers cyclists and joggers a picturesque view of the waterway.

Waterway Terraces

Yet, there might not have been a waterway had things gone according to plan.

The original Punggol 21 plan announced in 1996 did not feature a waterway. The Asian Financial Crisis in 1997 derailed that plan, as the economic recession dampened housing demand and put the Punggol vision on hold.

But the plan resurfaced in 2007 – bigger and better. Prime Minister Lee Hsien Loong announced Punggol 21 Plus at the National Day Rally, and the new town development was revived.

The waterway was then introduced as a key green and blue feature instrumental to transforming Punggol into a sustainable waterfront housing town.

Today, besides offering scenic views, the waterway also brings the community together with a constant flow of recreational activities. Residents are able to kayak in some areas and make use of the cycling and jogging route that runs adjacent to the water.

A town plaza, located in front of the main shopping mall Waterway Point, directly next to the widest bend of the waterway, serves as a congregation point for residents to rest, relax, and play.

Two rivers, Sungei Punggol and Sungei Serangoon, were dammed up to form two new reservoirs under the Punggol-Serangoon Reservoir Scheme. Because the reservoirs had to be linked to maximise storage capacity and for water transfer, using underground pipes was seen as an efficient solution, but a boring one. Instead, the waterway served up a novel – albeit more complicated – way of connecting the two reservoirs.

Like most other aesthetic features that HDB introduces, the waterway also serves important practical functions that contribute towards a more sustainable and greener Punggol, bringing added value to residents and visitors alike.

A scenic view of developments along Punggol Waterway.

biodiversity in the area was boosted by about

20%

with a wider variety of wildlife

A study done in collaboration with the National University of Singapore (NUS) showed that the design of the waterway facilitates wind flow in Punggol, acting as a major corridor to usher in a refreshing breeze.

Along some parts of the waterway, vertical green walls also help to mitigate built-up heat by reducing heat absorption on concrete.

A floating wetland system, designed in-house and made up of individual units locked in a honeycomb structure, was added to the waterway to introduce wetland species such as the water canna (*Thalia dealbata*), umbrella plant (*Cyperus alternifolius*), and denseflower knotweed (*Polygonum glabrum*). As parts of the waterway are used by residents for kayaking and canoeing activities, the water has to be kept consistently clean. Here, the plants' ability to remove pollutants and stabilise undesirable substances, using a natural process called phytoremediation, has helped to improve water quality.

As a result, biodiversity in the area was also boosted by about 20 percent, with a wider variety of wildlife, from birds to dragonflies and crustaceans, making a home for themselves along the waterway.

My Waterway@Punggol was the name eventually chosen by a focus group of 1,200 Singaporeans. The project to construct a river from scratch was an impressive engineering feat and demonstrated an inventive bent, creating a more refreshing living environment for residents.

The waterway even helped HDB clinch its first international award for environmental sustainability, presented by the American Academy of Environmental Engineers.

A man-made marvel

LOOKING at how residents have a splashing good time while kayaking at parts of the Punggol Waterway today, it may be hard to believe that the area was once an uninhabitable marsh land.

When Mr Chua Kok Eng first tested the soil conditions at the site prior to construction, he realised that the existing peaty soil and marine clay might present a challenge to getting the project off on a firm footing.

"The soil was soft like toothpaste. Anything built on it would sink," said the Director (Infrastructure and Reclamation).

Mr Chua and his team of engineers considered many alternatives before deciding on a sustainable and cost-effective solution that involved strengthening the soft soil. This was done by mixing it with cement and water injected into the ground.

But there were more obstacles ahead.

A combination of on-site challenges, time pressure, and the newness of the project meant My Waterway@ Punggol was no easy feat for the engineers.

For instance, the process of creating a river required digging as deep as five storeys at some parts. But the project's proximity to the existing Punggol MRT station posed a challenge to such massive digging.

"We had to ensure our construction did not cause any movement to the nearby MRT station and LRT viaduct structures by more than 1.5 cm – the width of a finger," said Mr Chua, adding that extensive feasibility studies had to be done prior to construction.

Even after that, the construction process had to be closely monitored to ensure the works were carried out with engineering precision.

About 3.3 million cubic metres of earth was eventually dug up – enough to fill 1,300 Olympic-size pools.

HDB reused all the excavated earth to fill the low-lying areas in Punggol Town, preparing the sites for future development.

For HDB, this 'cut and fill' approach was a green construction method that reduced the cost of transportation and disposal, and helped save about $40 million in construction costs.

Mr Chua Kok Eng, Director (Infrastructure and Reclamation), and Mr Wilfred Neo, Deputy Director (Infrastructure Engineering)

Aerators, jet fountains, and water curtains help to improve water quality and promote aquatic life.

There was still work to be done after the waterway was filled with water – specifically, 200 Olympic-size pools' worth of water.

Left on its own, the water could become stagnant and breed unsightly algae.

HDB conducted water quality studies and found the solution in jet fountains, aerators, and water curtains, which were then installed at strategic locations along the waterway.

More than just a sight to behold at night, the water management features circulated water and increased the oxygen levels in it. This has helped to improve water quality and promote aquatic life.

Under the supervision of Mr Wilfred Neo, Deputy Director (Infrastructure Engineering), the $225 million man-made marvel of a project was completed in 2011, after just two and a half years. Mr Neo played an important role in ensuring that the waterway was built on time and within budget, amid the myriad challenges.

HDB also worked closely with various government agencies to conceptualise and landscape the wider area. The aim was to promote urban water sustainability for Punggol Town, and enhance the living environment.

My Waterway@Punggol has become the embodiment of 'Green Living by the Waters' today.

Noting how flats along the waterway have become highly sought after, Mr Neo feels a huge sense of achievement. **"The numerous international and local accolades received are a testament to HDB's innovative spirit and commitment to creating vibrant and sustainable towns."**

Making a splash: Surveying residents living along the waterway

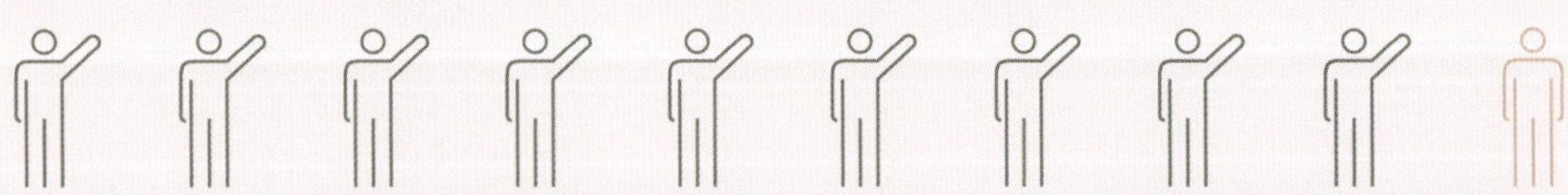

9 in 10

Residents felt the waterway added vibrancy to the town

Residents visited the waterway

Residents were satisfied with the waterway. The main reasons were:

- It made for a unique living experience
- It offered a nice view to enjoy
- It offered a nice place to exercise and relax

LINING THE BANKS WITH CHARACTER

Creating a river was just the start.

The next step was to inject vibrancy to the waterway with a ground-breaking housing concept that would cut through the tide of monotony.

The Waterway Terraces development represents HDB's efforts to seamlessly extend the waterscape towards the residential blocks on the riverbank. To carry out this vision, it organised a design competition that attracted 108 submissions from international and local architectural firms.

According to the competition brief, the homes would ideally have **"forms that respond to the water, maximising the views towards the waterway"**.

This was encapsulated by the winning entry which sought to amplify natural light and ventilation – a prime example of green architecture.

Today, the 1,876 homes also benefit from green features such as solar-powered lights in common areas, as well as compost bins and separate recycling refuse chutes.

today, the

1,876

homes in Waterway Terraces benefit from green features such as solar-powered lights in common areas, compost bins, and separate recycling refuse chutes

The terraced design of the roof gardens offers visitors and residents panoramic views of the waterway.

Capturing their love for Waterway Terraces

SIX days a week, Mr Josh Lim and his wife Chloe get their hands dirty and grimy in a noisy car workshop where they run their automobile business. But once they step back home, all is instantly tranquil.

"We spend the whole day facing machinery, so it's nice to come home to fresh air after a day of hard work," said Mr Lim, whose 4-room flat at the Waterway Terraces boasts a serene view of the man-made river.

The couple, in their 30s, was so thrilled with their new home that they had their wedding pictures professionally taken at their block's sky garden on the 18th floor. The stunning views of the town in the pictures are a result of the cleverly designed open terraces.

Mrs Lim was also excited to point out that their block is part of the Punggol waterscape featured in the pages of the Singapore passport as a background watermark.

"It's very meaningful to us, that it was chosen as one of Singapore's landmarks," she said.

Then newlyweds Josh and Chloe Lim took their wedding photos against the stunning backdrop of Waterway Terraces.

Terrace design: A step ahead of the competition

A mix of Singaporean ingenuity and Swiss design proved to be the winning formula for the landmark Waterway Terraces development.

Group8asia, a Swiss-based firm, had partnered Singapore-based Aedas to come up with a plan that linked the buildings, spaces, and water edges.

Their project design was lauded for its terraced housing form, beating 107 other design entries in HDB's design competition.

"By creating different tiers, opportunities were created for interesting garden designs, additional spaces for facilities and interactions, with spaces unique to this precinct," said the judging panel.

Waterway Terraces' design maximises the number of units that face the waterway, the courtyards, or the palm gardens – each offering residents a scenic view.

The rooftop spaces also provide residents with a **"bird's eye perspective of the whole waterway promenade, strengthening the connection between the people and the waterway environment"**.

The undulating design of the balconies at Waterway Terraces shields the units from heat and rain.

GREENING TOWNS THROUGH DATA

FROM large parks and small paths lined with plants to playgrounds and multi-storey car parks, greenery makes up a big part of HDB towns. But like a beautiful flower arrangement, it takes a team with careful and artful planning to put these green spaces together.

For HDB, it has been a process of continual improvement to provide more and better designed greenery, while ensuring the features can be well-maintained.

Mr Brian Low, Director (Landscape and Design), and his team oversee the landscape and greenery provision at HDB towns and estates, as well as the design and provision of facilities within green spaces. These facilities include playgrounds, fitness stations, and shelters, which balance the density of high-rise living. Requirements are in place to ensure sufficient greenery, including more mature trees.

The intention is for the outdoor environment to have various layers of greenery, from larger trees at the ground level to elevated skyrise greenery and community gardens at the rooftops.

It is also about carefully managing and curating natural elements so that they do not become an annoyance. Flowering plants are pretty when they bloom, but maintenance is an issue when flowers wilt and end up on the footpath.

"It's like how some people love butterflies but don't like to see caterpillars. So we keep the plants that caterpillars feed on away from the footpaths," noted Mr Low. **"Instead, we bring plants that butterflies like closer to the footpaths so people can enjoy and appreciate them. This brings them closer to nature, step by step."**

Mr Low also shared the importance of the human touch when it comes to planning for green spaces at HDB towns. Inevitably, he thinks of his two children, aged six and 14, and what types of playgrounds they would like.

For his team of landscape architects, more attention is now paid to the play value of HDB playgrounds to make sure they are fun and engaging. Thematic playgrounds have also been introduced to draw reference from the historical background or characteristics of the town.

TOP: SkyVille @ Dawson was planned with lush greenery and community spaces such as the rooftop gardens, while retaining elements of its heritage.

BOTTOM: Mr Brian Low, Director (Landscape and Design), at a military-themed playground in Choa Chu Kang, which pays homage to the army camps that once occupied the area.

HDB BIOPHILIC TOWN FRAMEWORK

Creating and maintaining the lush greenery in HDB neighbourhoods is a complex process that goes beyond how things look.

"It is not just about aesthetics," said Mr Wan Khin Wai, Director (Urban Design and Development). **"It is also about how you take care of the land and our natural assets when you develop the housing estate."**

An important question to consider is: How can HDB maximise the benefits of the natural system to alleviate the effects of climate change, while creating a high-quality environment for residents to enjoy?

Mr Wan and his team take reference from the HDB Biophilic Town Framework that looks at five key aspects: people, flora and fauna, outdoor comfort, water, and soil. Strategies under the framework include utilising trees and plants to serve multiple functions such as improving air quality, stormwater management, and heat mitigation.

Taken together, the framework promotes a greater sense of place and better well-being, and enhances the quality of life for residents.

For instance, to integrate nature into the daily lives of residents at the upcoming Northshore District, HDB has studied how to enhance the

Lush greenery surrounding Treelodge@Punggol **(TOP)** and Waterway Sunray **(BOTTOM)**.

five key aspects of the HDB Biophilic Town Framework:

People, Flora and Fauna, Outdoor Comfort, Water, and Soil

ecological connectivity between the existing natural habitat and its accompanying terrain and topography.

Using the data from the studies, green corridors were planned for the whole Punggol Town and extended to surrounding islands such as Coney Island, Pulau Ubin, and even the Straits of Johor. This will promote greater biodiversity and increase opportunities for residents to reconnect with nature and enjoy its therapeutic effects.

Once the green corridors are implemented, new habitats, such as dragonfly ponds, bird sanctuaries, and butterfly gardens, will be introduced for biodiversity to thrive. For example, trees such as the weeping willow tree (*Salix babylonica*) will be planted to attract the leopard butterfly, a species found in the area.

The next step would be to encourage residents to interact with nature at their doorstep by making the outdoor environment comfortable, so that they can explore and experience its restorative effect.

HDB Biophilic Town Framework

INTRODUCED:
2013,
updated in 2018

WHAT IT DOES:
Biophilia refers to mankind's innate affinity for and connection with the natural world. The framework outlines the principles and strategies for optimal planning and design of neighbourhood landscapes to enable people to enjoy nature's intrinsic benefits.

Key features and benefits:

SOIL

Managing and protecting a critical element of the landscape to support ecosystem processes such as plant growth and nutrient retention.

FLORA & FAUNA

Creating an environment that promotes good ecological balance with functional ecosystems.

OUTDOOR COMFORT

Optimising micro-climatic conditions and environmental factors such as temperature, wind, and noise to maximise residents' physical well-being outdoors.

WATER

Using principles in natural hydrology and the water cycle that are essential in promoting sustainable and resilient landscapes.

PEOPLE

Enhancing socio-cultural benefits and promoting physical and mental well-being by enabling people to reconnect, learn, and create with nature.

With the help of wind simulation studies, footpaths will be aligned with the wind flow pattern to maximise breeze for a pleasant walking experience. A sun study has also been carried out to determine shaded areas for garden trails, and habitat and activity zones, like playgrounds and fitness corners, to entice residents to explore their neighbourhood. The sun study was also used to identify areas with greater sunlight exposure for amenities that require it such as the community gardens.

On top of greening the environment and harnessing the benefits, the Biophilic Town Framework also looks at how stormwater management can enhance the living experience of residents. A district-wide network of vegetated bioswales and rain gardens has been incorporated for effective stormwater management, filtering out sediments and treating the rainwater run-off naturally.

As all these are done behind the scenes, residents may not realise how much work goes behind the beautiful greenery that adorns each town and estate. Each species of plant and how it is positioned is planned to a tee to ensure the best results for the best environment.

These measures reflect how HDB has progressed in its sustainability efforts through the years, aided by science and technology. Where trees were previously planted merely for shade, they are now chosen for their effectiveness in air quality management. Where water bodies were once placed for visual impact, they are now crucial in improving biodiversity.

Smart HDB Town Framework

Artist's impression of the aerial view of Punggol Northshore District.

INTRODUCED:
2014,
updated in 2017

WHAT IT DOES:
Shows how smart initiatives create a more liveable, efficient, sustainable, and safer living environment.

Key features:

SMART PLANNING

Computer simulation and data analytics help planners understand the environmental impact of their designs, thereby optimising resident comfort. For example, computer modelling tools are used to simulate wind flows in HDB towns. At a more detailed level, simulations help designers study how rain screens can reduce the amount of rainwater entering a community space.

SMART ENVIRONMENT

Sensors are installed to capture real-time information on the environment. For example, these sensors can be used to activate smart fans in Northshore District's Neighbourhood Centres in response to human traffic, temperature, and humidity. This results in more comfortable HDB towns for residents while reducing energy use.

SMART LIVING

Digital infrastructure installed in flats allows residents to adopt smart home solutions such as smart lighting and smart security devices. Without this, multiple gateways would have to be installed to bridge the solutions to home internet connections, which can be a hassle.

SMART COMMUNITY

Mobile apps can be developed for the community to build a digital ecosystem that generates data and creates new insight for HDB to better understand residents' needs. For example, anonymised data on shopping patterns can help HDB to better plan for the types of shops in a town.

SMART ESTATE

Sensors are used to detect faults in estate services such as obstructions within the Pneumatic Waste Conveyance System (PWCS), issues in the water pumps, and faults in the lifts. This enables contractors and the Town Councils to respond faster to incidents, thereby improving the reliability of estate services and reducing inconvenience to residents. At the same time, HDB collects performance data to study trends and develop predictive models, giving Town Councils greater insight into refining estate management.

ADVANCED MODELLING

From temperature to wind flow, noise, and human traffic, urban planners have many things to consider when developing an HDB neighbourhood. These factors affect where facilities are located or how buildings are constructed.

All these can be easily captured using technology, which aids the planning process.

One example is the Integrated Environmental Modeller (IEM), developed jointly by HDB and the Agency for Science, Technology and Research (A*STAR).

This advanced modelling tool uses high-resolution 3D city models to simulate conditions and their combined effects in an urban setting. It is part of 'smart planning' – one of the five key domains under the Smart HDB Town Framework. With the IEM, urban planners can better understand environmental factors to optimise the design of urban spaces.

The new Tengah Town is being planned using this tool. Concrete, vegetation, and water bodies will all be captured in the high-tech simulation, allowing planners to best design open spaces and optimise building layouts and orientation.

The IEM builds on the design technology that HDB has been developing through the years. Before this, Treelodge@Punggol, completed in 2010, was the first HDB project to be planned using simulation tools that optimise environmental factors such as wind flow. This paved the way for such simulation to be used for developments in new towns and estates.

The IEM tool is also impacting the lives of Singapore's youngest residents. It is used to ensure optimal placement of playgrounds and outdoor facilities to achieve a biophilic town. This method enables HDB to set aside shaded lawns outside childcare centres for outdoor lessons, where possible, even before construction starts.

"Outdoor spaces that are cooling, where kids can sit on the turf or tree stumps, really reduce the gap between man and nature," said Mr Brian Low, Director (Landscape and Design).

INTEGRATED ENVIRONMENTAL MODELLER (IEM)

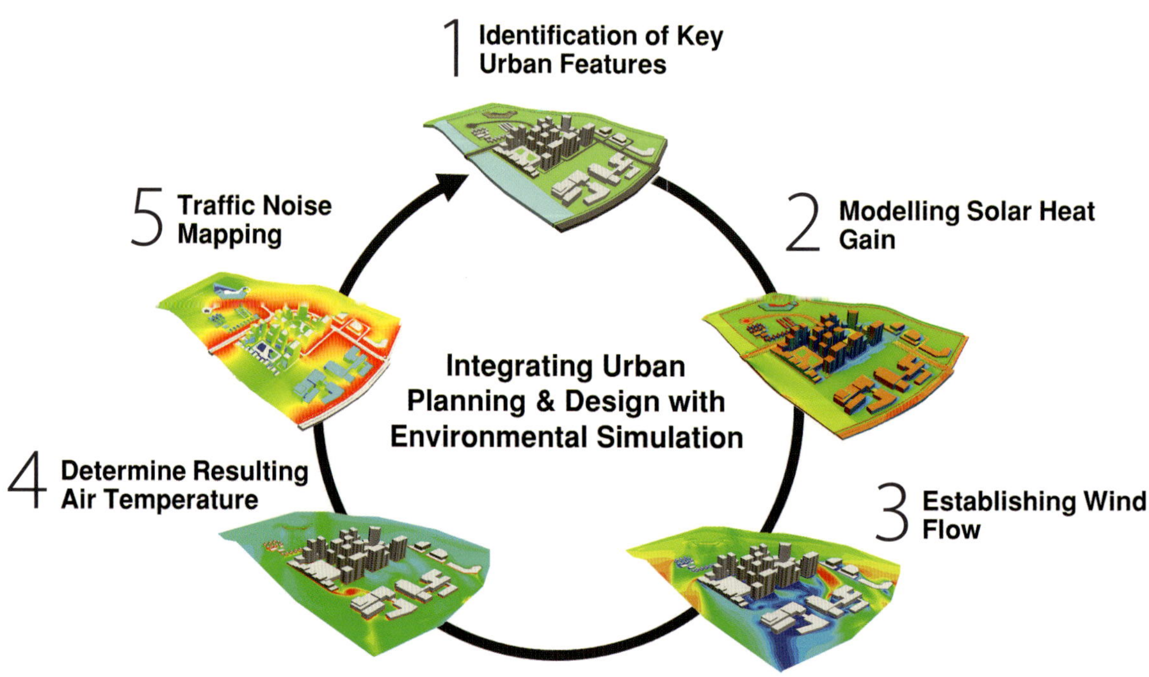

HDB's first eco-precinct greens the way

AT Treelodge@Punggol, vertical greening runs down the columns of the blocks and trees emerge from the basement car parks as means to lower temperatures.

But HDB's first eco-precinct is not just green on the outside. It is also green on the inside, as a sustainable way of life is encouraged.

When it was completed in 2010, Treelodge@Punggol was one of the first projects to be designed with recycling chutes at every floor – now a common feature for many new Build-To-Order (BTO) projects. General waste is thrown down another chute. As a result, the recyclables collected increased by three times.

Green technologies were also introduced in the precinct on an unprecedented scale, with many features replicated in later public housing projects.

The precinct was the first to be planned with the help of wind flow simulation to capitalise on prevailing winds to maximise natural cross ventilation. The result? A wind tunnel that flows through the spine of the Eco-Deck, which links all precinct amenities together including the car park roof, double-deck pavilion, playground, fitness corner, and community garden.

Every single detail was carefully planned, with studies carried out on how to cool the development at the precinct, block, and unit levels. The successful outcome paved the way for the simulation tool to be used in other Punggol developments and new areas like Bidadari.

Green technologies have also boosted energy and water management. The solar energy harnessed by solar panels on the rooftop is used to power common services such as the blocks' lights, lifts, and pumps, while motion sensors placed at staircases and car parks reduce energy consumption. All lifts include an energy regenerative system that recovers energy generated from lift braking. Rainwater collected from the rooftop is harvested for common area washing and irrigation.

It is perhaps apt that HDB's millionth flat since the statutory board's founding in 1960 was built in Treelodge@Punggol, which has helped to usher in a new green way of life for many Singaporeans.

The central Eco-Deck at Treelodge@ Punggol links all precinct amenities and also acts as a natural wind tunnel.

High-tech and green: The best of both worlds

Artist's impression of the aerial view of the green environment of Northshore District.

THE scenic seafront district of Punggol Northshore, which will be completed from 2020 onwards, is a first on many fronts, having incorporated new smart technologies and biophilic design concepts right from the start.

Making green design a breeze

Enter Northshore District and you will find ample shaded areas for gathering and a lulling breeze flowing through the neighbourhood. All these are not by chance, but by clever design.

During the design process, environmental modelling tools were used to simulate the microclimatic conditions of Northshore District, drilling down to details such as wind flow, temperature, and shadow casting. The result? The location and orientation of buildings capitalise on natural wind flow.

Careful thought was also given to the location of solar panels. Solar simulation was used to identify areas that receive extensive natural sunlight, so that solar panels can be planned for installation at these sites.

Northshore District was also the first district to adopt the integrated design strategies under the HDB Biophilic Town Framework. As a result, Northshore District comprises a greener environment that leverages the natural ability of greenery to improve residents' well-being.

Close collaboration by a multi-disciplinary team of engineers and architects was required to create this living environment. For example, flowering plants and trees were planted to attract butterflies, which in turn helped to pollinate plants at the street level, landscape deck, and even high up in the sky terraces. Guided by wind simulation studies, trees, such as the Tanjong tree, were planted along the main roads to help trap urban pollutants and make the air cleaner for residents to enjoy.

Lighting up for a safer, energy-efficient district

At Northshore District, lamp posts will not just light up the streets but also help prevent traffic accidents. The district will be the first to have smart lamp posts installed at selected areas. Using sensors to transmit data, these lamp posts will be able to detect fast-moving objects such as bicycles on the pavements or cars approaching the road junctions. Warnings are then triggered on the displays of the lamp posts to alert pedestrians.

The common areas will have smart lighting that automatically dims the LED brightness level when no motion is detected. This could save up to 60 percent more energy compared with conventional LED lighting. The motion data collected by the sensors can also be used to study movement patterns across various parts of the district, providing insights for better design of common spaces in the future.

Artist's impression of the street level view at Northshore District.

Artist's impression of residents enjoying the waterfront view at Northshore District.

A seamless, connected lifestyle

With just a smartphone, Northshore District residents can look forward to receiving detailed information of their households' energy usage anytime, anywhere by downloading the home energy monitoring app provided by the service provider. This is all thanks to smart technologies, such as Smart Sockets and the Smart Distribution Board, that are being piloted at selected precincts to support the tracking of energy consumed by the household.

This will encourage a more eco-conscious lifestyle among HDB residents. The Smart Distribution Board allows them to link compatible third-party solutions, such as smart lighting, smart security devices, and motion sensors, without the need to install multiple gateways. Adopting smart home solutions will be easier and more affordable.

For drivers, a smart car park will monitor parking demand, freeing up more parking spaces for visitors during non-peak hours. This means visitors will no longer be confined to parking on the higher floors of the multi-storey car park at non-peak hours, a hassle-free experience for all.

FULL SPEED AHEAD TOWARDS SUSTAINABILITY

AS a big organisation with more than 5,000 staff, HDB has been delivering quality housing to millions of Singaporeans for decades. But the challenge today is for HDB to find ways to be nimble and agile – must-haves in an age of technology and disruption – as it continues on its innovation journey.

HDB is likened to a powerful aircraft carrier, steadily delivering its massive building programme and projects. But to effectively develop and deliver cutting-edge technology with speed, HDB has introduced many 'speedboats' where various departments are encouraged to set up multi-disciplinary teams to carry out research and trial ideas. One such 'speedboat', at the Group level, is the Building & Research Institute (BRI), set up in 2009 to chart new waters in research.

Piloting this speedboat is Group Director, Er Dr Johnny Wong, who led his team to develop a comprehensive Research & Development Framework that guides all aspects of research within HDB, from pre- to post-construction. This ensures that any technology introduced addresses a real need, and that there is no duplication of resources or disproportionate spending on a particular area. It also helps teams to formulate a clear idea of the objective for each research project and how to achieve it.

One challenge the BRI team faces is resistance when introducing something new to an existing process, as that always carries some risks. **"That's where we need a never-give-up attitude to build trust, and a collaborative mindset with other HDB Groups,"** said Er Dr Wong.

To overcome such concerns, BRI would not only carry out research but also implement new ideas to projects that they have to design and execute in-house. This allows teething issues to be ironed out and proves that the new ideas work. Once successful, it would be easier to convince others to roll out the new initiatives to other projects.

The success stories speak for themselves, with BRI having garnered numerous awards both locally and on the international stage.

Besides embracing technology to drive future plans for new developments, there is also a need to rejuvenate existing HDB towns and estates with sustainable features, where possible. The HDB Greenprint programme does this by making existing neighbourhoods smart and sustainable through initiatives in the areas of waste management, and energy and water conservation.

Er Dr Johnny Wong, Group Director (Building & Research Institute)

the HDB Greenprint programme was extended to 40 blocks in Teck Ghee estate in 2015, benefitting about

5,800 households

In 2012, the HDB Greenprint programme was piloted at Yuhua estate in Jurong, where 38 blocks of flats of about 3,200 households were retrofitted with the PWCS, and rooftop greenery was introduced to reduce block surface temperatures by up to 1.6 degrees C.

Building on the sustainable improvements implemented in Yuhua under the HDB Greenprint programme, HDB introduced smart initiatives – some of which included Smart Waste Sensors, Smart Locks, and Smart Solar Energy Monitoring System – in a move to realise Singapore's Smart Nation vision. The HDB Greenprint programme was then extended to 40 blocks in Teck Ghee estate in 2015, benefitting another 5,800 households.

To build on the Greenprint effort, the HDB Green Towns programme was introduced in 2020. The programme is an ambitious 10-year plan to bring sustainable living to all existing HDB towns, with large-scale implementation of green features to improve residents' quality of life. It will focus on three areas of sustainability and liveability: reducing energy consumption, recycling rainwater, and cooling HDB towns.

Since 2005, HDB has been driving sustainability efforts to achieve a 10 percent reduction in HDB towns' annual energy consumption by 2020. By 2030, HDB aims to further reduce energy consumption in its towns by 15 percent from 2020.

Smart from the start

HDB has a suite of smart solutions for towns and estates that are rolled out from the moment the first excavator sets foot on the site to when residents start living in the homes.

Planning Smart

HDB has more than one million flats housing most of Singapore's resident population. Imagine harnessing all that data about HDB living which informs ways to improve the HDB experience for residents, remarked Er Dr Johnny Wong from BRI.

His team is doing precisely that with the Smart Hub – a data repository billed as 'the nerve centre of HDB'. With its operations centre layout and huge screens, it looks more like a place for space mission control than a regular office.

Through sensors planted in towns and estates, the Smart Hub collects real-time data on the performance of services such as lighting, lifts, and waste collection. This means predictive maintenance of lifts, for example, can be done. The objective is to be able to identify, uncover, and rectify potential issues and anomalies before a major breakdown occurs.

The Smart Hub is complemented by the Smart Urban Habitat Master Plan, a comprehensive digital master plan for each town that identifies where technology can be used for better living.

The first such plan was drawn up for Punggol in collaboration with private sector consultants, highlighting challenges for smart solutions and areas where more research is needed.

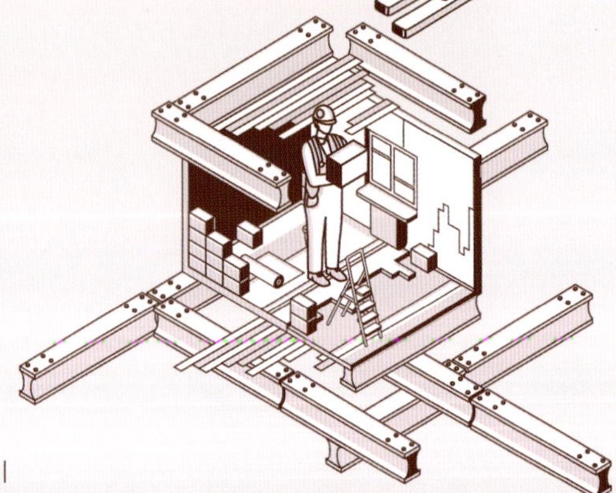

Building Smart

Many of HDB's smart solutions precede its Smart HDB Town Framework. One of the earliest was its precast technology.

Some HDB projects in the early 1980s already utilised precast concrete components such as beams, frames, and walls. Now, HDB has its own brand of semi-precast system tailored to Singapore's environment, improving labour productivity, quality control, and worksite safety.

Close to three-quarters of a typical HDB block's concrete structure is prefabricated today. HDB has also built prefabricated bathroom units. In addition, more than a third of new flats have adopted the Prefabricated Prefinished Volumetric Construction (PPVC) method since 2019. This means that the bathroom and bedroom units of the flat are prefabricated off-site, before being hoisted and stacked up progressively, like Lego bricks. Finishes like tiling can also be done off-site, which has improved construction productivity and the quality of finishes significantly.

The HDB Smart Hub, which collects real-time data on estate services such as lighting, lifts, and waste collection, is the 'brain' for operations at HDB estates.

Living Smart

All along, HDB has practised good passive design by orientating its blocks to minimise the number of West-facing units, which tend to receive unwanted heat from the sun, and to capture good wind flow. The Smart HDB Town Framework leverages new technology to enable residents to live even more comfortably and adopt greener lifestyles.

To make daily living in an HDB town more seamless and sustainable, sensors are installed in buildings to monitor performance and help in reducing water and energy usage.

No space is spared. Even basement car parks are planned with sensors to monitor the mechanical ventilation system, ensuring that carbon monoxide fumes from vehicles do not build up to unsafe levels. With this data, the mechanical ventilation system can then be scheduled to run only when required, reaping further energy savings. This system will be piloted in the Northshore District, and subsequently in all car parks in Tengah and Punggol that require mechanical ventilation.

It is not just young digital natives who benefit from smart technology. The Elderly Monitoring System was piloted in Yuhua where sensors were installed in the homes of seniors, especially those who lived alone, to monitor their well-being. The seniors' caregivers would receive text messages in the event of irregular patterns in the seniors' behaviour.

Mr Yee Yung Kong, a senior resident who was one of the trial users, found the Elderly Monitoring System useful and convenient. **"If an accident happens at home, my children will be notified immediately,"** he was quoted saying in media. He also felt that this system should be installed in more households so that family members and caregivers can effortlessly monitor the well-being of seniors at home.

Other users felt the same way. At the end of the trial, more than 80 percent of users found that it gave them better peace of mind. In addition, the trials helped small- and medium-sized businesses and telcos better package their solutions with more competitive pricing, making it more affordable for residents to adopt smart home solutions.

Powering sector-leading research

The Centre of Building Research spearheads HDB's R&D efforts in building and environmental sustainability, while nurturing new technologies for future generations of public housing. L-R: Mr Chew Jia Han, Ms Emiko Lim, Mdm Teh Poh Suan.

IN a nondescript corner of Woodlands lies HDB's master laboratory, or BRI's 'playground'. The Centre of Building Research (CBR) extends across two buildings, complete with office space, training facilities, and a four-storey production area.

There is ample space for all kinds of research and development (R&D) to be tested and applied.

A large grey concrete structure is located prominently on the ground floor, which has high ceilings in a factory-like setting. This centrepiece is a room fabricated through 3D concrete printing – one technology HDB is tinkering with. Next to the printed room is a 3D concrete printer – said to be the largest in Southeast Asia.

Further down to the precast production yard is the PPVC mock-up. Here is where designers and researchers simulate the installation process, especially the in-house developed connection systems focusing on constructability, robustness, and flexibility in stitching the modules together.

Next to the PPVC mock-up, there is the Automated Precast Production System (APPS), which improves the precast production process by integrating Computer Aided Design Drafting & Manufacturing (CAD/CAM) capability into the production process. This makes it easier to produce a greater variety of customised precast components while reducing the demand for manual labour, allowing for more complex designs to be fabricated and installed quickly.

Move up a couple of floors and you are greeted by what look like HDB flat showrooms – except these are 'concept apartments' that feature new ideas in a unit layout. They are used to test-bed alternative building materials for fixtures and finishes, the soundproofing quality of doors and windows, and noise mitigation technologies. Smart home technologies are plugged in and thoroughly tested before being introduced to HDB flats.

Up on the roof are various types of solar panels as well as different species of plants. Research on suitable plants that require minimum maintenance is done using the patented Prefabricated Extensive Green Roof Tray System, or PEG trays, which are lightweight and portable. The system has proved a standard-setter for the industry, and has even been exported to Hong Kong.

CBR is symbolic of HDB's innovation journey. The building had started out as the Prefabrication Technology Centre in 1995, used mainly as a factory that churned out new precast concrete components with the pioneering technology of the time.

While retaining elements of the precast factory, the building was rebranded as CBR in 2009 to spearhead HDB's R&D efforts in building sustainable towns, in sync with the subsequent Roadmap to Better Living in HDB Towns.

At CBR, the team is able to conduct in-house research to identify new technology and weave it into HDB's housing projects in a cost-effective way. In this manner, HDB continues to set proven standards, passing them on to the private sector consultants who are designing the housing projects.

Hence, by supporting a rigorous process, from R&D to test-bedding and the introduction of new urban solutions to new HDB towns and estates, CBR has played and will continue to play a central role in Singapore's housing journey, bridging theoretical findings with practical applications.

This has proven to be a winning formula for the BRI speedboat in navigating the unchartered seas of innovation.

Leveraging APPS technology to automate production processes.
L-R: Mr Chew Keng Keong, Mr Chang Tze Lum, Mr Koh Guan Bian.

REMAKING HEARTLANDS, RENEWING ESTATES

IT was early 2007, and Dr Chong Fook Loong and his team were up to their necks in work to give three HDB towns – Punggol, Yishun, and Dawson – a makeover, under the Remaking Our Heartland (ROH) programme.

"It was an incredible, humongous amount of effort," said Dr Chong. The towns selected for ROH were of various age profiles – intentionally selected for this variety. As each town had distinct characteristics, the proposals had to be customised: relatively new Punggol, with its waterway; mature Dawson, with its 'housing-in-a-park' concept; and middle-aged Yishun, with a focus on town centre connectivity and upgrading works.

There have since been three phases of ROH involving nine towns. The programme forms just one aspect of HDB's sustainability agency, which works in unison with other rejuvenation plans to keep towns updated.

When ROH was launched in 2007, two other upgrading programmes were also announced to benefit older precincts across the island. The Home Improvement Programme (HIP) is aimed at addressing issues in ageing flats, while the Neighbourhood Renewal Programme (NRP) focuses on upgrading the common areas. Flat owners in a middle-aged town like Yishun are beneficiaries of such programmes.

ROH and various upgrading programmes play a key role in ensuring that existing HDB towns continue to enjoy improvements and are able to sustain a quality living environment for its residents.

The Punggol Master Planning Team at the rooftop of Oasis Terraces, overlooking Waterway Ridges. L-R: Ms Lim Fang Ting, Ms Wong Si Min, Ms Corrinne Lim, Group Director (Research & Planning) Dr Chong Fook Loong, Ms Stephanie Loh, Ms Pebble Lee, Ms Chin Ming Li, Ms Chantalle Goh.

Wow, is this really public housing?

PERHAPS the most drastic makeover for an HDB estate is exemplified by Dawson – an ageing 60-year-old estate that was given more than a nip and tuck. It underwent a major facelift.

Mr Chua Gim Teck recalls the first birthday celebration of his son, Cheng Feng, fondly. It was a large family gathering of almost 50 people on the 36th floor sky garden in SkyVille @ Dawson, right outside their unit.

Stepping into the sky garden, with towering pillars artistically strewn along the perimeter, one feels as if the Singapore cityscape is right at your feet. Sentosa and the Singapore Strait beckon on one side, gleaming skyscrapers at the Central Business District glimmer at the other.

"We had a nice unblocked view of the city, and everyone was enjoying themselves chit-chatting and having drinks," he said. **"But the wind was very, very strong,"** Mr Chua added with a laugh.

It is hard to imagine that the simplest low-rise flats – one of the earliest public housing projects built in Singapore in the 1950s – used to be located in Dawson, before making way for stylish 40-storey blocks with panoramic views.

Sky gardens were incorporated in Dawson's ROH programme to improve the living environment of the area. As a prominent feature of HDB's new public housing projects, this concept is being replicated in the upcoming areas in Punggol and Tampines.

The project, SkyVille @ Dawson, designed by local architectural firm WOHA, also includes other green features like rooftop solar cells, bioswales, and rubbish chutes for recyclables.

Even as HDB pushed frontiers, it was also important for Dawson to retain its heritage and character – a crucial aspect of ROH. There are murals depicting bygone days – such as children fishing in small streams – on the ground floor walls of SkyVille @ Dawson.

Mr Chua enjoys the murals, and often sees groups on heritage tours in the estate. **"It is nice to know this place has some history. Sometimes when we walk past murals, we will tell our son about what it depicts,"** he said.

It is this sort of old-school identity, coupled with the latest technology, that really sustains the lifeblood of an HDB estate. The amalgamation of the old and the new ensures that generations upon generations are able to enjoy and live comfortably through the life cycle of an estate.

Mr Yap Chin Beng, former Deputy Chief Executive Officer (Estate & Corporate) and Senior Advisor (Estate & Corporate), with the Dawson ROH Team at SkyVille @ Dawson. L-R: Mr Derek Loei, Mr Yang Chun Chiat, Ms Yvonne Yee, Mr Yap, Ms Kathleen Goh, Mrs Lee-Loy Kwee Wah, Ms Cheng Ya Ling.

Upgrading programmes

Continual improvement

LIFT UPGRADING PROGRAMME

The Lift Upgrading Programme (LUP) was introduced in 2001 to offer direct lift services to flats where it is technically and financially feasible. Besides providing residents with more convenient access, the lifts also benefit the seniors, families with young children, and the less mobile.

"The lifts will provide me with ease of access to my home when I age in later years. Right now, my elderly mother, who comes over frequently, is very happy to use the lifts instead of the stairs," shared Madam Shiremi, whose block at Queen's Close has undergone the LUP.

The scope of works includes the upgrading of existing lifts, the provision of a lift landing on every floor, and the addition of new lifts and lift shafts. LUP is a massive programme and has cost the Government about $5 billion in total. Since its launch, over 500,000 flats have benefitted from LUP.

NEIGHBOURHOOD RENEWAL PROGRAMME

Another programme put in place in 2007 was the Neighbourhood Renewal Programme (NRP), which focuses on block and precinct improvements. It is implemented on a 'neighbourhood' basis, across two or more precincts. This allows improvements to be carried out more comprehensively, with better coordination and integration.

It also ensures that improvements across neighbouring precincts complement each other. Some of the popular improvements include covered linkways, drop-off porches, playgrounds, fitness stations, and seating areas at void decks.

A key feature of the programme is the active engagement of residents in shaping their living environment. This is carried out through a two-stage consultation process – Public Consultation and Consensus Gathering. At least 75 percent of the residents must support NRP before it can be implemented.

In 2014, NRP was extended to include blocks built up to 1995, benefitting an additional 100,000 flats. When the programme was first introduced, priority had been given to flats built before 1989.

The scope of NRP was also expanded to include various improvement works, such as the repair of spalling concrete and apron drains and floors, and the re-screeding of void deck and corridor floors. This ensures that neighbourhoods are rejuvenated in a more comprehensive and coordinated manner, and residents will not be inconvenienced twice because Town Councils will not have to carry out the works separately from NRP.

As at December 2019, 79 NRP projects have been completed, benefitting some 116,000 flats.

HOME IMPROVEMENT PROGRAMME

Announced in 2007, the Home Improvement Programme (HIP) focuses on improvements within the flat and helps residents deal with common maintenance problems related to ageing flats in a systematic and comprehensive manner. There are three main components of works under HIP: Essential, Optional, and Enhancement for Active Seniors.

Essential improvements, such as repairing spalling concrete and structural cracks, are considered necessary for public health, safety, and technical reasons. Residents may also opt for the optional improvement items such as toilet upgrading, new decorative door, and refuse chute hopper.

HIP was initially offered to flats built up to 1986. In August 2018, Prime Minister Lee Hsien Loong announced the extension of the programme to flats built between 1987 and 1997.

Some 320,000 HDB flats have been selected for HIP, and another 230,000 more HDB households will benefit from the extension.

In addition, every HDB flat can expect to be upgraded twice during its 99-year lease – once when they are about 30 years old, through HIP, and a second round when they reach around 60 to 70 years old, under HIP II.

ENHANCEMENT FOR ACTIVE SENIORS PROGRAMME

The Enhancement for Active Seniors (EASE) programme was launched in July 2012 to enhance the safety and comfort of seniors living in HDB flats. Improvements include grab bars, slip-resistant treatment to existing bathroom flooring and ramps to negotiate level differences inside the flat and at the main entrance.

EASE is offered in conjunction with HIP so that the works under both programmes can be carried out at the same time. Residents who need the EASE improvements earlier can apply directly to HDB.

As at December 2019, about 146,250 households have opted for EASE together with HIP, and over 77,000 households have directly applied for EASE.

"EASE improvement items go a long way in helping seniors age in place and giving peace of mind to their family members," said Senior Estate Manager Tan Chiew Yan from the Home Improvement & Building Services Section, Housing Maintenance Department.

"It is heartening and rewarding to know from the seniors that their quality of life has improved as they are now able to move around the flat more confidently. Seniors also need not worry as EASE improvement items are heavily subsidised by the Government."

SERS: Estate rejuvenation scheme in the midst of renewal

Mr Yap Chin Beng, former Deputy Chief Executive Officer (Estate & Corporate) and Senior Advisor (Estate & Corporate), at Tanglin Halt estate, which was announced for redevelopment under the Selective En bloc Redevelopment Scheme.

THE Selective En bloc Redevelopment Scheme (SERS) is one of the hardest schemes to implement, revealed Mr Yap Chin Beng, former Deputy Chief Executive Officer (Estate & Corporate) and Senior Advisor (Estate & Corporate).

Under the scheme, which started in 1995, flats chosen for SERS are redeveloped to optimise the use of land, and residents are rehoused en masse at designated replacement flats nearby. It is part of the Government's Estate Renewal Strategy to selectively rejuvenate HDB estates with high redevelopment potential.

To some, having their flats announced for SERS may feel like striking the lottery, but others may feel concerned as they would have to uproot themselves from familiar surroundings.

"Acquiring the flat under SERS is compulsory because it's done through the Land Acquisition Act," said Mr Yap, who retired in 2019. **"[It is] to acquire people's flats, probably the most valuable asset the family has. The challenge for us is to hand-hold them through this entire process."**

The entire journey can take about six years, from the day SERS is announced to when residents move into their new homes.

Throughout their SERS journey, residents may experience various emotions, from initial anxiety to excitement when their new flats are completed.

Engaging the residents right from the start is therefore vital. There are dedicated HDB SERS Journey Managers to guide each SERS household through the various milestones such as the SERS Connect sessions, where residents will receive detailed financial counselling and advice on rehousing options.

But SERS has also helped to uplift lives, as residents are able to move from ageing flats into new homes with modern designs and comprehensive facilities – which is why Mr Yap remains most proud of the scheme through his storied 42-year career at HDB.

To retain the strong community ties built over the years, SERS residents are rehoused at replacement flats located near their existing homes wherever possible. There is also a special Joint Selection Scheme for up to six households to choose new flats together, so that they can live near each other.

The bonds among residents can help them forge a collective sense of ownership for their new homes, even as they retain fond memories of their old flats.

A good example was the replacement precinct at Commonwealth 10, which was used to rehouse about 700 families from Blocks 74 to 80 Commonwealth Drive. The site was announced for SERS on 8 August 2008. The precinct's name 'Commonwealth 10' was suggested by the residents themselves as the old flats in Tanglin Halt were 10-storeys high, and commonly known as *Chap Lau* (Hokkien for '10 storeys').

On the whole, SERS is a popular scheme. Past surveys have found that 85 percent to 95 percent of SERS residents expressed strong support for the scheme.

Nevertheless, there are challenges to announcing many more flats for SERS, as it is limited to sites with high redevelopment potential. Many of such sites have already been announced for SERS, after more than 20 years of implementation.

Looking ahead, as HDB towns grow older, there will be a need to plan ahead and redevelop them in an orderly manner.

As announced by Prime Minister Lee Hsien Loong at the 2018 National Day Rally, a new Voluntary Early Redevelopment Scheme (VERS), will help to pace out the redevelopment of HDB towns over several decades.

VERS is a long-term plan to be implemented in about 20 years' time. HDB will continue to study the details of the scheme to progressively renew and transform towns for future generations.

Commonwealth 10 was the replacement precinct for about 700 families from Blocks 74 to 80 Commonwealth Drive.

ENSURING CONTINUITY

AS the threat of climate change looms overhead, HDB has a big part to play in ensuring that future generations do not just live in green homes, but also live green.

Sustainability is more than being earth-friendly. There are also social and economic facets, such as creating a vibrant community and an identity for towns, that help to fortify their character and longevity.

How do you sustain a town? It is a perennial challenge to house an ageing population with diverse and changing needs, but technology and tools are helping to accelerate this process of going green and smart to make HDB living more comfortable and convenient.

Sustainability also needs to be measured to be effective. Big Data, frameworks, and smart tools turn green efforts into a science. These resources quantify success objectively and offer a guide to planners and policy-makers in developing the best HDB towns.

All of this also has to be complemented with the human touch as housing is a deeply personal issue. Policies, such as SERS for instance, have to be delivered with tact and sensitivity.

It is a never-ending process in striving towards better homes for all. But the mission remains the same: To make public housing better for residents by providing affordable homes of quality and value.

Big Data, frameworks, and smart tools

turn green efforts into a science

The new generation of public housing, such as Treelodge@Punggol **(TOP)** and Waterway Terraces **(RIGHT)**, is testament to HDB's commitment to ensure towns remain highly liveable and sustainable.

CHAPTER ④

BETTER TOGETHER

HOMES FOR EVERYONE, IN CLOSER AND CONNECTED COMMUNITIES

> HDB has a very important social role – to ensure that you have a roof over your head. As much as possible, we will help you to own a flat. Home ownership provides a greater sense of stability and community.

Mr Mike Chan
Deputy Chief Executive Officer (Estate)

As a growing city, Singapore is constantly shifting and adapting to change. The traditional *kampungs* of wooden, zinc-roofed houses – often with no running water or electricity – that once dotted the island have since evolved into modern green towns with high-rise Housing and Development Board (HDB) blocks.

But the *kampung* spirit lives on. This, in fact, is one reason why HDB's public housing model is one of the world's most successful public housing programmes.

For many Singaporeans, this shared sense of belonging, social camaraderie, and cohesion is what makes a house a home.

Beyond building homes and planning towns, HDB has another critical role to play. Well-designed, smart, and sustainable towns have to be undergirded by solid housing polices and strong communities.

In this respect, HDB's work runs on two important tracks. One revolves around policy-making, which focuses on measures relating to home ownership, strengthening family ties, and meeting the needs of different groups of people. The other centres on community-building efforts aimed at creating a connected living environment to forge deeper bonds among residents.

To fulfil HDB's vision of creating a better living environment and meeting the evolving lifestyle aspirations of Singaporeans, as outlined in its Roadmap to Better Living in HDB Towns, these two tracks have to move in tandem.

POLICY-MAKING

HOME OWNERSHIP: AN UNCHANGING GOAL

The residential neighbourhoods of Commonwealth and Tanglin Halt in the early days.

PERCHED on a hill in Commonwealth Close, Block 81 was a breath of fresh air in the 1960s, set apart from the typical 10-storey flats at the time by its long, simple slab design.

Together with nearby blocks, residents referred to the 16-storey building affectionately as *Chap Lak Lau* (Hokkien for '16 storeys').

On one particular afternoon in February 1965, it was not the estate that drew the crowds, but the opportunity for a rare glimpse of British royalty. Word had gotten out that His Royal Highness Prince Philip, the Duke of Edinburgh, was stopping by the estate to look at how HDB provides public housing.

Block 81 had become an icon of Singapore's public housing programme. It was one of the first few blocks to be put up for public sale under HDB's then newly-minted Home Ownership for the People Scheme launched in 1964. Prior to that, all HDB flats were for rent only.

The scheme was mooted by the late Mr Lee Kuan Yew, who was convinced that home ownership would give every citizen a meaningful stake in the nation. In the decades that followed, Singapore's founding Prime Minister continued to reiterate his conviction. In 2011, he said: **"Our families own their homes and are rooted to Singapore. Owning their homes gives everybody a sense of ownership."**

The drive towards home ownership underpins HDB's continual efforts to make public housing affordable and accessible to all Singaporeans. It has successfully turned Singapore into a nation of proud flat owners, contributing to economic, social, and political stability. Today, about 80 percent of the Singapore resident population live in HDB flats across the island. Of these households, about nine in 10 own the flats they live in.

Existing measures continue to be tweaked to better meet the diverse needs of different segments of the

Block 81 Commonwealth Close earned the moniker 'VIP Block' (VIP as short for 'Very Important Person') for hosting foreign dignitaries from His Royal Highness Prince Philip to United States Vice President Spiro Agnew, as well as former Japan Emperor Akihito when he was the Crown Prince.

population, including vulnerable groups. More schemes have also been introduced to encourage parents and their married children to live with or close to each other for mutual care and support.

In all of this, HDB has stuck closely to its goal from the start: To create meaningful, vibrant, and cohesive HDB living through the simple yet powerful idea of home ownership.

in **2008**, Singapore's Home Ownership for the People Scheme received the

United Nations Public Service Award

RISING ABOVE POLICY-MAKING CHALLENGES IN TIMES OF CHANGE

THE last decade has been characterised by a constant stream of changes. Lifestyles and expectations in Singapore have continued to shift. Adding to that, volatility has become a norm across global markets, and economic cycles are much shorter.

As a result, policy-making at HDB has become far more complicated, particularly in relation to home ownership.

Take the subprime mortgage crisis that hit the United States in 2008 as an example. It triggered a full-blown Global Financial Crisis, and even though Singapore was quick to recover from the recession, it faced another problem soon after: A red-hot property market.

Young couples and families were finding it more challenging to purchase a flat as property prices rose quickly, fuelled by a flood of liquidity and strong demand.

HDB moved quickly and with tenacity. It also ramped up the supply of new flats through its Build-To-Order (BTO) programme, from about 9,000 units in 2009 to about 16,000 units in 2010.

A total of about 100,000 new BTO flats were then launched for sale between 2011 and 2014. The prices of these new flats were pegged to rates that were substantially lower than that of resale flats, owing to a higher government subsidy, so that new flats remained affordable to first-timer households.

HDB also began to take a more proactive stance in stabilising the HDB resale market, which included measures to tighten liquidity by collaborating with other agencies such as the Monetary Authority of Singapore (MAS).

At the same time, Group Director (Estate Administration & Property) Ms Tan Chew Ling, and her team worked on formulating and refining its policies to better cater to different segments of the population, from first-time flat buyers and seniors, to singles and the vulnerable.

The changes then were shaped by an extensive consultation exercise in 2012, as part of Our Singapore Conversation (OSC), a national dialogue that allowed organisations like HDB and the Ministry of National Development (MND) to better understand ground sentiment and address specific concerns by fine tuning policies.

Formulating such policies and putting them into action had been anything but easy. **"We did not know if the policy changes would be effective, or how far-reaching the impact would be. But we couldn't afford to have that bubble. That was where social and policy intervention had to come in,"** recalled Ms Tan.

The efforts paid off. Between 2009 and 2014, BTO flat prices in non-mature estates rose by just 15 percent (without grants). Measured against the household income increase of 38 percent over the same period, this marked a huge improvement in public housing affordability.

One thing is clear: Amid change and heightened volatility, policy-making at HDB has become far more sophisticated, yet still unwaveringly focused on building a stable, home-owning society.

In Singapore, where housing is both an economic and a social good, HDB continues to perform the delicate balancing act of taking care of the needs of flat owners, while managing the vicissitudes of the market.

The following section will look at three key areas in which HDB sought to meet the needs of different groups of people, with policies that:

- Provide **an affordable and accessible** home for every family, from first-timers to the low-income;
- Build **an inclusive home** for all by taking care of the needs of different buyer groups such as young couples, seniors, singles, and divorcees;
- Foster **closer and stronger family ties** by encouraging family members to live together or close to one another.

Ms Tan Chew Ling, Group Director (Estate Administration & Property), and her team continually review and refine policies to cater to different segments of the population. L-R: Ms Norlilah Bte Abdul Latiff, Mr Loh Swee Heng, Ms Tan Hui Kuan, Mr Ignatius Lourdesamy, Ms Tan, Ms Lily Wong, Ms Phee Peck Shang, Mr Daniel Chan.

AN AFFORDABLE AND ACCESSIBLE HOME FOR EVERY FAMILY

AT HDB, home ownership has always been a key priority that is grounded in two thrusts: Affordability and accessibility.

Since 2010, HDB has offered more housing grants and raised income ceilings several times to keep up with the rising incomes of citizens – all with the objective of making public housing more affordable and accessible to a wider group of people.

Today, many are able to use their CPF savings to service their mortgage with minimal or no cash outlay. The mortgage servicing ratio for first-timer families buying new flats in non-mature estates is generally under 25 percent, well below the international benchmarks for affordable housing of around 30 to 35 percent.

There are a number of schemes and grants in place to help first-time flat buyers own their new homes.

HELPING SINGAPOREANS BUY THEIR FIRST HOME

HDB's priority is the first-timers. Eligible families can buy a flat from either HDB or the resale market.

First-timers can tap on a plethora of schemes to secure their HDB flat. New flats are priced with significant market discounts, and generous housing grants are offered to help them own their first home.

The **Enhanced CPF Housing Grant (EHG)** introduced in September 2019 marks the latest milestone, where buyers of either a new or resale flat can qualify for a grant of up to $80,000. For a first-timer buying a BTO flat, the EHG is offered on top of a market discount.

First-timers buying resale flats get to enjoy the CPF Housing Grant, the EHG, and the Proximity Housing Grant (PHG). Together, these grants can add up to $160,000.

Beyond financial assistance, other schemes are in place to help first-timer flat buyers such as the **Parenthood Provisional Housing Scheme (PPHS)** and the **Parenthood Priority Scheme (PPS)**.

WHAT
Enhanced CPF Housing Grant (EHG)

WHEN
2019

HOW MUCH
Up to $80,000

HOW IT WORKS
It supports first-timer households with an average gross monthly income of $9,000 or less over a 12-month period preceding the flat application.

Available to those buying a new or resale flat of any type and in any location.

WHAT
Parenthood Provisional Housing Scheme (PPHS)

WHEN
2013

HOW MUCH
Rental rates for a 3-room or 4-room flat start from $600, lower than market rates

HOW IT WORKS
It provides interim housing for married and fiancé-fiancée couples comprising at least one first-timer, and divorced/widowed persons with children who are waiting for their new HDB flats to be completed.

From November 2014, a maximum of two families are allowed to co-rent the flat. This helps families who do not require a whole flat for temporary accommodation and wish to save some money.

PARENTHOOD PROVISIONAL HOUSING SCHEME (PPHS)

PPHS babies

MUST a couple have an HDB flat first, before they can have a baby?

The answer, according to Minister for Manpower and Second Minister for Home Affairs Ms Josephine Teo[1], is quite simple: No.

"Couples need not wait until their BTO flats are ready before marrying or having a child," she wrote in a Facebook post in January 2016, citing the Parenthood Provisional Housing Scheme (PPHS), which provides a temporary rental option in an HDB setting.

As part of the National Population and Talent Division's (NPTD) enhanced Marriage & Parenthood package, HDB launched 1,150 flats for application in January 2013 under the PPHS. The aim was to provide temporary housing for first-timer married couples with children below 16 years old as they await the completion of their new HDB flats.

The scheme was revised twice in April and September 2013 to benefit more families such as couples who were expecting.

And the cherry on top of the icing, added Ms Teo, was the indirect and unintended effect of encouraging couples to start a family earlier in silvering Singapore: **"Here's the best part – since PPHS became available, nearly 230 babies have been born to couples living in these flats!"**

The number has only grown since. As at the end of December 2019, some 740 babies were born to PPHS households during their stay in these flats.

1 Josephine Teo was Senior Minister of State, Prime Minister's Office (PMO), overseeing the National Population and Talent Division (NPTD) and Senior Minister of State for Transport in 2016.

Flats in Blocks 189 and 190 Boon Lay Drive are rented out under the Parenthood Provisional Housing Scheme.

ENHANCED CPF HOUSING GRANT (EHG)

Three makes a family

Ms Michelle Lee and her family making new memories in their home in Woodlands Crescent.

IT took four pregnancy tests in a single day before Ms Michelle Lee was finally convinced the result was accurate: She was pregnant.

Disbelief, and then elation. After all, a doctor had told her before that she would be unable to conceive due to a health issue.

"I remember I told my husband outside the toilet in a shopping mall, and he just shouted, in front of everyone, 'I'm going to be a dad!'" she recalled, laughing.

Ms Lee and her husband, Mr Lim Xian Xing, welcomed their baby boy, Kaius, in July 2019. He is nicknamed '*mantou*' for his round face, and because of Ms Lee's constant craving for the Chinese steamed bun during her pregnancy.

The family of three moved into their new nest at Woodlands Crescent in January 2020 – a 3-room resale flat close to Ms Lee's parents' home in Sembawang, where they were staying previously, and her own workplace. Helped by grants such as the Enhanced CPF Housing Grant (EHG) and the Proximity Housing Grant (PHG), they forked out about $178,000 for the flat.

For Ms Lee and Mr Lim, the grants were a big help. Every dollar counts for a young family starting out like them.

"It was quite a special feeling – that we actually have a place of our own now, even though our lives have changed a lot," Ms Lee said, smiling as she looked over at baby Kaius, now seven months old.

"This time last year, my friends would call me out to hang out at night, and I'd go without thinking twice. Now I have to tell them I can't, because I have to look after my baby at home. So it's true, our lives have changed a lot, but I wouldn't have it any other way."

SPECIAL CPF HOUSING GRANT (SHG)

My house, my rules

IMMEDIATELY after collecting the keys to their BTO flat in August 2019, Madam Suriana Saleh and her husband, Mr Mohamad Taufiq, rushed to their new home in Canberra Crescent for a first look.

For them, the mere act of setting foot into the empty flat brought a feeling of warmth and excitement.

"That feeling of standing in our own house was surreal," shared Madam Suriana.

She and her husband are now proud owners of a 4-room BTO flat at EastLink II @ Canberra – a dream home purchase that was only made possible with HDB's Special CPF Housing Grant (SHG). They received a grant amount of $20,000, paying about $270,000 for the flat.

The SHG and the Additional CPF Housing Grant (AHG) were two grants that played key roles in ensuring housing affordability before the EHG was conceived. The SHG provided eligible families with additional assistance of up to $40,000 in buying their first BTO flat (4-room or smaller) in non-mature estates, while the AHG of up to $40,000 was open to those buying either a BTO or resale flat.

Both schemes were discontinued when the EHG was introduced in 2019 to further improve affordability for prospective HDB flat owners.

"Having stayed with my parents all along, I can finally say now that it is 'my house, my rules'," added Madam Suriana, whose family of three – the couple has a two-year-old son – moved in in February 2020.

"I love how our flat is breezy, and it faces away from the afternoon sun. It also helps that we are just a 10-minute drive away from either of our parents, and the new Canberra MRT station is just five minutes away on foot."

Madam Suriana Saleh and her husband, Mr Mohamad Taufiq, bought their first home in Canberra Crescent with the help of the Special CPF Housing Grant.

RAISING THE INCOME CEILING FOR GREATER ACCESSIBILITY

While HDB is committed to helping citizen families own a home, it also has to ensure that housing subsidies are given to those who need them most. To do so, HDB sets an income ceiling as a form of means-testing, and reaches out to targeted household segments for the purchase of subsidised HDB flats.

In line with this, it has continually reviewed and raised income ceiling requirements through the years to make its affordable housing options more accessible to flat buyers.

In 2019, the monthly household income ceiling was raised from $12,000 to $14,000 for eligible families to:

- **Buy a flat from HDB;**
- **Buy a resale flat on the open market with a CPF Housing Grant;**
- **Get an HDB housing loan for the purchase of a new or resale flat.**

The monthly household income ceiling for eligible first-timer singles, aged 35 and above, was also correspondingly raised from $6,000 to $7,000.

The monthly household income ceiling for a family buying an Executive Condominium unit from a property developer was increased to $16,000.

$14,000 PER MONTH	$7,000 PER MONTH
FOR A FAMILY BUYING:	**FOR A SINGLE BUYING:**
A new flat	A new 2-room Flexi flat (99-year lease) in a non-mature estate
A resale flat on the open market with CPF Housing Grant	A resale flat (up to 5-room) on the open market with CPF Housing Grant

HELPING LOW-INCOME FAMILIES FIND STABILITY

For families who are not yet able to own their homes, HDB offers rental flats with heavily subsidised rental rates. But the ultimate goal remains the same: Home ownership.

"Owning a flat is quite different from renting one," said Deputy Chief Executive Officer (Estate), Mr Mike Chan. **"Home ownership provides a greater sense of stability."**

Between 2015 and 2019, some 4,700 tenants of HDB rental flats have moved on to own their homes with the help of various HDB housing schemes and grants.

More work is under way to help rental tenants fulfil their aspiration of owning a home. In 2019, the Home ownership Support Team (HST) was set up to guide families who are ready for home ownership, but may be unfamiliar with the policies and processes involved.

The HST guides rental households through their entire home ownership journey, from planning their home purchase to when they collect the keys and settle in their new home. When working with families, the HST seeks to understand the circumstances of each family, such as their housing needs, financial health, employment stability, and other pressing priorities, and creates a plan with them towards home ownership.

The HST aims to reach out to 1,000 rental households by 2023, helping more people progress towards home ownership.

Two initiatives are also in place to help second-timer families living in public rental flats own their homes: the **Step-Up CPF Housing Grant**, which was introduced in 2013 and later enhanced in 2019, along with the **Fresh Start Housing Scheme** in 2016.

WHAT
Step-Up CPF Housing Grant

WHEN
2013, enhanced in 2019

HOW MUCH
$15,000

HOW IT WORKS
This grant is given to second-timer families residing in 2-room flats who wish to upgrade to 3-room new flats in non-mature estates.

Since May 2019, it has been expanded to include those buying 3-room resale flats in the non-mature estates, as well as second-timer families living in public rental flats and buying 2- or 3-room new or resale flats in the non-mature estates.

WHAT
Fresh Start Housing Scheme

WHEN
2016

HOW IT WORKS
Second-timer families with young children who are living in public rental flats can tap on this scheme with a housing grant of $35,000.

It assists them in owning a 2-room Flexi flat with a shorter lease, while integrating financial assistance with personal responsibility and social support.

RENTAL TO HOME OWNERSHIP WITH CPF HOUSING GRANTS

From tenant to proud flat owner

Mr Kelvin Ng @ Abdullah Ng and his family in their new 3-room BTO flat.

FOR Mr Kelvin Ng @ Abdullah Ng, moving into a brand new BTO flat at Bukit Batok West Avenue 9 marked a big milestone.

He and his family had been staying in a 2-room public rental flat in Teck Whye Crescent for six years, before making the upgrade to their current 3-room BTO flat.

HDB staff had approached him from three years ago, checking in regularly to see if he and his wife, Madam Zuraidah Bte Sudarmaji, were financially ready to progress to owning their own home.

To help with the purchase, which was about $180,000, the couple received a combination of the Additional and Special CPF Housing Grants amounting to $70,000. They and their two children, aged 10 and eight, moved into the flat in 2019.

"It's better to have our own house, and we can pay for it by CPF," said Madam Zuraidah. **"We have a lot more space now,"** said Mr Ng, adding that this will be useful for his two children. **"It's better to have a house that belongs to us."**

AN INCLUSIVE HOME FOR ALL

AN outstanding city, as former Minister for National Development Mr Lawrence Wong said in 2018, is not just economically attractive but also inclusive – a place that embraces diversity, where different social groups mix and have equal opportunities to participate.

This is why housing plans in Singapore must continually evolve to encourage a more equal and inclusive society, and take care of the needs of various groups.

Against the backdrop of Singapore's ageing population, a growing number of singles, and a widening income gap, HDB has introduced more targeted policies aimed at meeting the increasingly diverse needs of Singaporeans over the last decade.

This means working towards leaving no one behind, so that everybody – from first-time flat owners and seniors to singles and divorcees, as well as the low-income and vulnerable – is able to have a home of their own.

For greater convenience, seniors can opt for kitchen cabinets under the Optional Component Scheme.

TAKING CARE OF THE SENIORS

Like many other developed economies, the rapidly ageing population in Singapore has become a key concern in recent years, especially with more Singaporeans living longer today. The city-state's average life expectancy of 83.6 years is one of the highest in the world.

To support the needs of seniors, HDB has adopted a multi-pronged approach, starting with the provision of senior-friendly flats.

Launched in 1998, the Studio Apartment (SA) Scheme offered seniors aged 55 years and above an additional housing option. The SA Scheme also provided an alternative for seniors to monetise their existing property. They could sell their existing property, move to an SA, and use the sale proceeds to supplement their retirement income.

The 2-room Flexi flats are available in sizes ranging from 36 sq m to 46 sq m.

These SAs were specially designed and customised for independent living. They were conveniently located within established towns, with easy access to transport and amenities. Sold with 30-year leases, they came in move-in condition, with fittings like kitchen cabinets, a cooker hob and hood, wardrobes, as well as elderly-friendly features such as grab bars, bigger switches, and an alert alarm system.

Cognisant of the changing housing needs, HDB introduced the **2-room Flexi Scheme** in 2015 to replace the SA and 2-room Schemes, catering to the diverse housing needs of families, singles, and seniors. The scheme incorporated feedback and suggestions received through extensive public consultation. The 2-room Flexi Scheme gives different buyers flexibility in the length of lease, as well as the fittings and finishes of their 2-room Flexi flat based on their age, needs, and preferences.

WHAT

2-room Flexi Scheme

WHEN

2015

HOW IT WORKS

It allows elderly citizens to buy a new flat with a lease best suited to their needs, instead of the full 99-year lease. The lease ranges from 15 to 45 years, in five-year increments, and has to cover the younger owner to at least 95 years old.

First- and second-timer families as well as first-timer singles can buy a new 2-room Flexi flat on a 99-year lease.

The flats are available in sizes ranging from 36 sq m to 46 sq m.

Buyers who purchase 2-room Flexi flats on 99-year leases can opt for flooring and sanitary fittings under the Optional Component Scheme (OCS).

Seniors who buy 2-room Flexi flats on short leases can choose from three OCS packages. The components include flooring, sanitary fittings, built-in kitchen cabinets with induction hob and cooker hood, kitchen sink, window grilles, and built-in wardrobe. The flats are also fitted with grab bars upfront.

The Lease Buyback Scheme allows seniors to monetise their flats to supplement their retirement income.

The rationale was clear: The needs of seniors, along with that of families and singles, were evolving. HDB had to respond.

Mr Yap Chin Beng, former Deputy Chief Executive Officer (Estate & Corporate) and Senior Advisor (Estate & Corporate) who retired in 2019, recalled when an elderly woman filed an appeal some years back to buy an SA on a shorter lease.

"I still remember she said this, 'I'm already 82 years old. Why must [the rules] still insist that I keep the flat for 30 years?'" he shared. **"That really prompted us to rethink the policy."**

Today, in total, 11,250 units[2] have been booked by buyers aged 55 and above.

Beyond providing housing, HDB has introduced a range of monetisation options, such as the **Lease Buyback Scheme (LBS)**, to allow seniors to tap on their flat to supplement their retirement income.

WHAT
Lease Buyback Scheme (LBS)

WHEN
2009

HOW IT WORKS
The LBS is designed to help elderly flat owners monetise their flat while continuing to live there.

Those aged 65 years and above can sell part of their flat's lease back to HDB, and choose to retain the length of lease based on the age of the youngest owner.

Proceeds from the sale will be used to top up their CPF Retirement Account. They can use this to join CPF LIFE, which will provide them with a monthly income for life.

The LBS was previously only available to owners of 4-room or smaller flats, but has been extended to owners of all flat types since January 2019.

The maximum cash bonus was increased across all flat types in March 2020.

2 Based on booking data from sales launches between November 2015 and May 2019, 10,314 units were sold on short leases, and 936 units on 99-year leases.

2-ROOM FLEXI SCHEME: SHORTER LEASE OPTIONS FOR SENIORS

Blossoming into the golden years

MS Lim Beng Guat likes to start her mornings on a fresh note – with an invigorating walk at the Bukit Gombak Stadium, right next to the scenic Little Guilin Park in Bukit Batok.

The simple routine keeps the spritely 70-year-old going, be it helping to cook for her grandchildren, or carrying out her part-time work at fast-food restaurants at least four days a week.

"I like to keep myself busy," Ms Lim said in Mandarin, smiling.

She had moved into her 2-room Flexi flat at the nearby Bukit Gombak Vista in June 2018. The flat came with a lease of 35 years, helped by CPF housing grants totalling some $20,000.

Living in her own home has given Ms Lim a newfound sense of freedom and independence to do what she wants, including pursuing her own hobbies in her own time.

Besides being able to wake up to a view of greenery every morning, Ms Lim is also grateful for her friendly neighbours, who have never hesitated to lend her a helping hand such as fixing the clock in her house.

"These may all be little things, but I'm really very happy," she said.

The 2-room Flexi Scheme allows seniors to buy a flat on a shorter lease, ranging from 15 to 45 years, in five-year increments.

HDB will introduce public housing that is integrated with care services to help seniors age in place.

A NEW TYPE OF LIVING FOR SENIORS

As more seniors look for alternative residential options, Singapore has announced plans to introduce the first assisted living public housing development for seniors in Bukit Batok.

The new flat typology integrates public housing with care services under a service package to help seniors age in place.

The pilot development will comprise more than 160 units and boast large communal spaces on every floor of each block. The units, at about 32 sq m each, will be enhanced with senior-friendly fittings, larger bathrooms, and features that accommodate those with mobility needs.

OPENING MORE DOORS FOR SINGLES AND DIVORCEES

Seniors are not the only ones who have benefitted from policy changes.

For the first time in 2013, singles aged 35 years and older were allowed to buy new 2-room flats in non-mature estates – a move that opened up more housing options for a group that otherwise could only buy resale flats.

When the scheme was first launched in July that year, there were more than 50 singles applying for one unit. HDB responded to the high demand by increasing the number of 2-room flats to be sold. The demand from singles has since eased.

To address the pain point for divorcees and their children, the rules were revised later that year for divorced couples to each own or be included as an essential occupier of a subsidised flat. The wait-out period was also reduced from five years to three years, before being lifted altogether in 2018.

2-ROOM FLEXI SCHEME: NEW HOMES FOR SINGLES

A new beginning

DEMAND for 2-room Flexi flats among singles was so hot at one point that more than 50 individuals were vying for one flat. Among them was independent film producer and trainer Juan Foo.

After three attempts to apply for a flat since 2013, he finally collected the keys to his new BTO flat in Bukit Batok West Avenue 6 in 2018.

"It was like a 'fresh start' to the next stage of my life. Hopefully a nice, quiet, and private place for me to live," said Mr Foo, 47, who had lived with his parents previously.

Getting a flat on the resale market had not been an option given that it was beyond his budget.

"Having a place of my own, using whatever resources I have to purchase it, also resonates with me as a Singaporean – that I can have an apartment in Singapore to call home," he added.

The 2-room Flexi Scheme opened up more housing possibilities for first-timer singles.

FOSTERING CLOSER FAMILIES, STRONGER TIES

WHEN the year-long OSC that involved 47,000 people in dialogue drew to a close in 2012, it threw up a salient finding: Singaporeans wanted the *kampung* spirit, encapsulating the notion of mutual support, to be kept alive.

Specifically, many wanted to live closer to their families to better care for and support one another.

To this end, HDB has listened and responded. It has continued to roll out and refine policies with the aim of facilitating and encouraging families to live together or close to one another for strong mutual care and support – to build ties that bind.

Living in HDB flats evokes a *kampung* spirit where families build camaraderie and offer mutual care and support.

KEEPING THE FAMILY TOGETHER

Facilitating mutual care and support is key to building strong familial ties.

Motivated in part by the insights drawn from OSC in 2012, the **Proximity Housing Grant (PHG)** was implemented in response to an increasing desire by Singaporeans to buy a resale flat to live with or near their parents or child.

Two other schemes that help married children and their parents to live with or near one another are the Married Child Priority Scheme (MCPS) and the Multi-Generation Priority Scheme (MGPS).

The MCPS helps a married child live with or close to the parents by improving the flat applicants' chances when they ballot for a new flat.

The MGPS differs slightly in that parents and their married child can make a joint application for two flats in a BTO project where 2-room Flexi or 3-room flats are included in the flat mix. Parents can apply for a 2-room Flexi or 3-room flat, while their married child's household can apply for a 2-room Flexi or larger flat.

For seniors who wish to buy a 2-room Flexi flat to age in place within a familiar environment, or to live near their parents or married child, the Senior Priority Scheme (SPS) can help improve their ballot chances. At least 40 percent of such flats offered during sales launches are set aside for senior applicants – of which half are for eligible applicants under the SPS.

Specially-designed flats, known as Three-Generation (3Gen) flats, were also rolled out in 2013 to help multi-generation families live under one roof. Each of these flats, at about 115 sq m, comes with four bedrooms and three bathrooms – of which two are en-suite – to provide extra room, comfort, and privacy for residents.

Initiatives such as the Proximity Housing Grant help families stay close together.

WHAT
Proximity Housing Grant (PHG)

WHEN
2015

HOW MUCH
Up to $30,000

HOW IT WORKS
The PHG was introduced to help more families buy a resale flat to live with or close to each other for mutual care and support.

From 2018, it encompasses a simplified proximity condition, defined as within 4 km of each other (previously defined as within 2 km or the same town).

It offers buyers of a resale flat a higher-tier grant of $30,000 to live with their parents or child, or $20,000 to live near them.

Eligible singles can also enjoy a PHG of $15,000 if they buy a resale flat to live with their parents, or $10,000 if they live near their parents.

PROXIMITY HOUSING GRANT (PHG)

A recipe for a happy family

SPREAD across the dining table is a colourful smorgasbord of home-cooked food: Steamed fish, stir-fried vegetables, sweet and sour pork, roast chicken, and a hearty soup.

But it is hardly Chinese New Year – just a regular weekday night.

Mrs Kelly Thong, 44, and her family are over at her mother's house for dinner, and the matriarch has whipped up a feast.

"When my mother cooks for two – just my father and herself – she always has 'no mood'," said Mrs Thong. **"But now that we're going over more often for meals, she's definitely much happier. And she never fails to throw in an extra dish or two for her grandkids, who love her cooking."**

Mrs Thong lives in a 5-room flat in Sengkang with her husband, three children, and parents-in-law – just two streets away from her parents.

She was one of over 28,000 households that have benefitted from the Proximity Housing Grant (PHG) since it was launched in August 2015. The grant was set up to encourage married couples, singles, and their parents to live nearby or together for mutual care and support.

When Mrs Thong and her family moved into their current flat in 2019 and invited her parents-in-law to live with them, they were able to tap on the PHG of $30,000.

Mrs Thong's parents were also beneficiaries of the PHG when they moved from Tampines to be near her.

"I've always been asking my mother to move closer to my sister (who lives in the Anchorvale area) and me. This struck home early last year, when my dad was unwell," she shared.

"My parents are both in their 70s. We want to take care of them if anything happens to them. Being just two streets away now, I can get to them in a five-minute drive instead of having to travel to Tampines. This will be very critical in times of emergency."

Of course, there are other advantages to living near her parents, she added.

"Whenever my mother travels, I'll have to go over and clean the house or water the plants," Mrs Thong said, laughing. **"But she comes over to clean up my place when we are away too."**

Living in close proximity means Mrs Kelly Thong (seated, second from right) and her family can easily enjoy many more meals with her parents, who live just two streets away.

MULTI-GENERATION PRIORITY SCHEME (MGPS)

Bonding over mahjong

The sound of *mahjong* tiles is a familiar one in the Hiah family. Mr Eric Hiah's parents often go to his place to have a game or two with him and his wife (centre).

ALMOST every weekend, Mr Eric Hiah's parents would go over to his house – two flats away – and the whole family would bond over one beloved activity: *Mahjong,* a popular Chinese tile-based game.

"We all love playing *mahjong,*" said Mr Hiah, 29, adding that his family can spend hours on end indulging in their favourite game. **"My wife and my mother are quite close, so it helps that we can easily spend time with one another just by walking over."**

It was through the Multi-Generation Priority Scheme (MGPS) that Mr Hiah and his wife, Madam Phua Hui Ngim, were able to live so close to his parents in the same block.

Both couples received the keys to their respective flats in November 2018, and moved into their new homes in July 2019.

"For us, it's really also about planning ahead. My parents are getting older, so when they need me, I can be there," Mr Hiah said. **"And if we have kids in the future, it will be a bonus if my parents can help."**

Under the Remaking Our Heartland programme, lifestyle hub Heartbeat@Bedok opened in 2018, housing various community facilities under one roof; while Bedok Town Centre **(RIGHT)** was transformed with a new town square and an enhanced pedestrian mall.

COMMUNITY BUILDING

BUILDING THE URBAN *KAMPUNG*

MUCH of HDB's work to build a closer and connected community in its towns and estates has gained momentum over the last decade.

More than just building homes, HDB has continued to bolster and further refine its community-centric efforts such that they work hand in hand with policies to create more inclusive and cohesive communities – the backbone of vibrant and colourful HDB living.

This second section will look at four key areas in which HDB has rolled out initiatives to build a modern-day *kampung* for all:

Fostering diverse and inclusive neighbourhoods for social harmony in the community;

Creating new spaces for interaction that enliven HDB living;

Reviving the heartland spark with rejuvenation plans for HDB towns, estates, and shops;

Empowering the community through the process of co-creation and active ground-up participation.

FOSTERING DIVERSE AND INCLUSIVE NEIGHBOURHOODS

Singapore's rich, multicultural social fabric was not something that came by chance, but one achieved through conscious and deliberate efforts aimed at fostering racial integration and inclusiveness.

The long-standing Ethnic Integration Policy (EIP) is one policy that has come into play in everyday lives. Introduced in 1989, the EIP's goal was to prevent the formation of ethnic enclaves, and foster integration by giving residents more opportunities to interact with different races.

The EIP limits are set at block and neighbourhood levels, which broadly reflect Singapore's ethnic make-up.

In March 2010, the Singapore Permanent Resident (SPR) quota was introduced for non-Malaysian SPRs to facilitate better integration of SPRs with local community and prevent enclaves. Hence, when buying an HDB resale flat, buyers are to ensure they are within the EIP proportion for the block and neighbourhood, and if applicable, the SPR quota as well.

These policies are put in place to ensure there is a balanced mix of ethnic and citizenship communities in HDB towns and estates. In the same vein, HDB has also stepped in to encourage interaction between households of different profiles.

Since 2008, rental blocks have been included within BTO projects, where they share the same facilities and amenities. These include BTO projects such as Punggol Edge, Keat Hong Colours, Oleander Breeze @ Yishun, and Tampines GreenRidges.

The Ethnic Integration Policy creates opportunities for residents of different backgrounds to come together.

At another four BTO projects – Marsiling Greenview, West Plains @ Bukit Batok, Fernvale Glades, and Costa Grove – both rental and sold flats were built within the same block.

To forge a shared spirit of neighbourliness and social harmony in the community, HDB has rolled out several programmes. These include the Good Neighbour Award, which recognises and honours residents who go the extra mile to enrich their community with exemplary acts of care and neighbourliness, as well as MyNiceHome roadshows, which help new flat owners learn more about their future homes and familiarise themselves with their new living environment.

GOOD NEIGHBOUR AWARD

Neighbours for life

"I'LL openly admit this: I am *kaypoh* about my neighbours," chuckled Madam Rasamal Nadayson, using a colloquial term that means 'busybody'.

"It's because I care. I love them so I always want to make sure that they are okay."

Affectionately known as Aunty Rose by her neighbours, Madam Rasamal can be seen making her rounds at the estate in Dover Road every day. The 83-year-old, who is fluent in Chinese dialects like Hokkien, Hakka, Cantonese, and Teochew, embodies the spirit of neighbourliness as she goes around visiting her neighbours, chatting and sharing food with them.

Among them was Ms Lim Mei Cheng, 33, and her elderly father. **"I had been living here for years, but we never spoke much. It wasn't until five years ago, when my father was admitted to the hospital, and she asked me where he was,"** Ms Lim recalled.

"At the time, I thought she was just another *kaypoh* auntie. But I was surprised when I visited my father in hospital the next day, and she was there."

Mr Lim, who has hypertension and diabetes, was able to return home after about five months at the hospital. But his condition did not improve, and dementia kicked in.

Madam Rasamal looked out for him. Knowing that he refuses to eat his meals properly, she would get an extra packet of chicken rice for him each time she buys food from the coffee shop. **"He particularly loves mooncakes so I used to get those for him too,"** she added.

For Ms Lim, or 'Ah Mei' as Madam Rasamal calls her, these small gestures have eased the load. **"To her it's nothing much, but to me, it means a lot,"** she said.

To show her appreciation, Ms Lim nominated Madam Rasamal for the Good Neighbour Award in 2019. The award, which was launched in 2009, aims to recognise and honour residents who have made a difference to their communities with their heart-warming acts of neighbourliness.

While Ms Lim and her father have shifted to their new home in Bukit Batok, she continues to call and visit Madam Rasamal regularly.

As for Madam Rasamal, everyone is family. "**When I see Ah Mei's father, it is like seeing a younger brother. I told both Ah Mei and her helper that anytime they need my help, they can always come and find me,"** she said.

When Ms Lim Mei Cheng's elderly father fell ill, their neighbour, Madam Rasamal Nadayson, helped look out for him and made sure he ate his meals on time.

CREATING NEW SPACES FOR INTERACTION

Having a shared and well-designed space is critical for the community to interact and come together in a meaningful way. Recent initiatives like the New Generation Town Plazas and the New Generation Neighbourhood Centres have boosted community-building efforts by providing residents with more focal and common spaces for engagement.

But work in such community-building efforts had started much earlier, even before the Roadmap was launched in 2011. In the early years, common corridors that link flats in every storey of an HDB block, for instance, were meant to simulate the close-knit *kampung* living of the olden days. Today, HDB is doing more.

To create meaningful communal spaces, well-thought out designs are pivotal. HDB is therefore mindful of the need to understand social behaviour in order to design spaces for people, be it for lively activities or some quiet time. This understanding led to the concept of a community living room as a welcoming space for residents to interact and bond with fellow neighbours.

These designated communal spaces are located in the void deck, and typically have views of the precinct landscaping and facilities. Tables and a variety of seats are provided to create a conducive space for residents to socialise with their neighbours in small groups.

HDB also recognises the importance of complementing design and infrastructure with programming to enhance community bonding and place identity. By collaborating with local community stakeholders, Activation Teams are formed to ensure that there is a steady slew of activities at these community plazas for the residents' enjoyment. In this way, a space is transformed into a place.

The mass workouts at Kampung Admiralty are a great way for residents to bond with one another, and keep fit and active.

REVIVING THE HEARTLAND SPARK

IN 2007, HDB rolled out the **Remaking Our Heartland (ROH)** programme as a comprehensive blueprint to spruce up existing towns and estates, so that the HDB heartland remains sustainable and vibrant, along with the **Revitalisation of Shops (ROS)** scheme to boost the vibrancy and competitiveness of HDB shops.

Besides improving the built environment of HDB neighbourhood centres, HDB also creates opportunities to improve the vibrancy of HDB neighbourhood centres.

HDB works closely with Enterprise Singapore and Heartland Enterprise Centre Singapore to implement place-making activities to help the Merchants' Associations (MA) garner support from stakeholders on the ground. MAs are independent entities that represent the interests of hawkers or shop owners when communicating with grassroots organisations, Town Councils, and government agencies including HDB.

Through active collaboration with the Institutes of Higher Learning and other government agencies, HDB has successfully brought together more than 400 students, agency partners, and the MAs to curate interesting events and activities for the neighbourhood centres.

Under the Lively Places Programme, which is a joint initiative by HDB and the Urban Redevelopment Authority (URA), HDB also serves as a bridge for MAs and shop owners to organise meaningful community projects at the neighbourhood centres such as performances for the Lunar New Year celebrations, Mid-Autumn Festival carnivals, karaoke sing-along sessions, mass exercises, and free meals for needy residents. There are plans in the pipeline to work with a consultant to roll out a series of place-making initiatives at some neighbourhood centres.

WHAT
Remaking Our Heartland (ROH)

WHEN
2007

HOW IT WORKS
The ROH maps out plans to renew HDB towns and estates. The aim is to meet the changing needs of the community, while capitalising on the unique characteristics of each area.

Punggol, Yishun, and Dawson were the first heartland towns and estates announced in 2007 to undergo ROH, followed by East Coast, Hougang, and Jurong Lake in 2011. Woodlands, Toa Payoh, and Pasir Ris were selected for ROH 3 in 2015. The fourth batch of towns to undergo ROH – Bukit Merah, Queenstown, Choa Chu Kang, and Ang Mo Kio – was announced in 2020.

WHAT
Revitalisation of Shops (ROS)

WHEN
2007

HOW IT WORKS
The ROS is part of HDB's measures to boost the vibrancy and competitiveness of HDB shops.

Where HDB retailers or the local Merchants' Associations (MA) are keen to spearhead revitalisation efforts, the ROS scheme can help retailers upgrade the shopping environment and carry out promotional events.

The scheme was enhanced in 2016 to provide shop owners with greater financial support.

REVITALISATION OF SHOPS (ROS)

Helping heartland shops stay fresh

MORE than three decades – that was how long shops at Jurong Central had gone without a major facelift.

"We just weren't successful in getting enough support or funds to carry out upgrading works through the ROS scheme," said Mr Roland Tan, Chairman of Jurong West Street 41 Merchants' Association.

"We were close to getting it done about five years ago, but then there was the fire, which really affected everyone in the area."

The fire, which happened in 2016, razed a wet market and coffee shop to the ground.

But in early 2019, a total of 105 shops at Jurong Central were able to emerge anew, with a fresh look, after having finally tapped on the HDB's ROS scheme.

Since November 2007, the ROS scheme has been in place to boost the competitiveness of heartland shops, so that they can better serve HDB residents.

In 2016, the Government delivered a major round of changes to the ROS, providing shop owners with greater financial support. This included raising the upgrading budget for each shop by 75 percent to $35,000, and reducing shop owners' share of the upgrading cost from 50 percent to 20 percent, capped at $5,000 per shop.

A new start-up fund of $10,000 was also introduced to encourage HDB shops without an MA to form one, along with a new fund of up to $10,000 for the associations to appoint consultants to help them with upgrading plans. More than 4,400 shops have benefitted from the scheme.

"At first, everybody was afraid to upgrade because they were fearful there would be no business. It's natural," said Mr Tan in Mandarin.

"But things are now much better than the past. The shops look nicer, the paths are wider, and the whole area is a lot brighter. All of this has attracted more people, and for us businesses, that's a good thing."

Mr Roland Tan, Chairman of Jurong West Street 41 Merchants' Association, helped push for upgrading efforts under the Revitalisation of Shops scheme, which have attracted more business to shops at Jurong Central.

REMAKING OUR HEARTLAND (ROH)

Remaking Bedok: From ageing to bustling town

IT was December 2013, and Bedok was bustling with Christmas cheer.

The swanky Bedok Mall had just opened, becoming the first major shopping mall in Bedok. Boasting popular brands like UNIQLO, Cotton On, and restaurant chains such as Din Tai Fung and Tim Ho Wan, the mall drew in crowds by the hundreds.

The mall's extensive offerings, prime location, and excellent connectivity to major transport nodes with its integrated bus interchange were setting it up to be **'the heart of Bedok Town'.**

Bedok was one of the towns selected for rejuvenation works under HDB's ROH 2 for East Coast, launched in 2011. The rejuvenation of Bedok Town Centre was one of several key proposals under the ROH programme, which harnessed the potential of the Bedok area to transform and refresh the living environment for existing residents. The new Bedok Mall was the result of these rejuvenation plans, aimed at giving the mature town a brand new lease of life.

Just a few steps away, the revamp of the surrounding Bedok Town Centre Pedestrian Mall was also under way. The installation of new ramps at the pedestrian mall made it easier for residents to get around.

Introduced at a time where foot traffic and sales were dwindling for many mom-and-pop shops there, this project was special. It was the first time HDB worked closely with local community stakeholders and residents to plan and implement 'place activation initiatives' – projects that could activate public spaces and streets to bring people together.

In place of the old food centre today is the new Bedok Town Square – HDB's first Town Plaza that was launched on 20 May 2016. Seamlessly connected to the new Bedok Interchange Hawker Centre that was built right next to it, Bedok Town Square houses popular local food stalls, and serves as a prominent gathering point for residents.

As HDB's first New Generation Town Plaza which prioritised community activities over commercial use, nearly all features of Bedok Town Square – from its unique theme to the types of events held there – were built with the community's inputs.

The result was greater community ownership and involvement, a deeper sense of identity and belonging, and a more active and cohesive community. The Heritage Corner, the first marker of the Bedok Heritage Trail, captures the long and rich history of the area to further strengthen the residents' understanding of their town.

With the new Heartbeat@Bedok, Singapore's second integrated community club that houses various public amenities under one roof, residents also enjoy greater convenience. The one-stop integrated lifestyle hub comprises a sports centre, a senior care centre, a polyclinic, a public library, a community club, childcare and enrichment centres, as well as retail and F&B outlets.

"When you come out from Bedok Mall, the first thing you see is the lively Town Square, and you can walk through the pedestrian mall to Heartbeat@Bedok. Everything is well-connected," explained Mr Khoo Hock Khim.

Formerly the Chairman of the Merchants' Association at Bedok Town Centre, Mr Khoo had been part of the committee involved in the ROH upgrading works at Bedok. **"The whole area is now much brighter, more vibrant. There's always something going on at any one time,"** he added.

The mature town of Bedok was given a new lease of life under the Remaking Our Heartland programme for East Coast.

Mr Khoo Hock Khim, former Chairman of the Merchants' Association at Bedok Town Centre.

EMPOWERING THE COMMUNITY

With the help of residents in the area, the once spartan void deck at Block 683C Woodlands Drive 62 has been transformed into an Instagram-worthy hang-out spot for residents of all ages.

BEING in a modern *kampung* goes well beyond having facilities at your doorstep.

As then Second Minister for National Development Mr Desmond Lee put it at the opening of the HDB Community Week in 2019: **"It is really all about relationships – the people, the friendly neighbours, and the warmth of the community."**

His comments encapsulated the increasingly collaborative approach that has taken precedence in HDB's community-centric efforts over the past decade, as it sought to engage residents more deeply for a stronger sense of belonging.

"HDB has always nurtured communities. But we can always do better, and particularly when people and their needs are changing," said Chief Executive Officer, Dr Cheong Koon Hean. **"We need to engage the residents such that they are able to proactively do something for the community themselves."**

An empty grass patch between Blocks 96 and 97 Aljunied Crescent has been enlivened and become more welcoming with play elements like swings and mini-gardens added by residents of Aljunied Crescent.

One early initiative was the Hello Neighbour! @ Tampines Central project, which was mooted in 2015 to test out new design ideas – converting void decks and common walkways into new social spaces – that are aimed at encouraging community bonding.

This followed an earlier study by the National University of Singapore (NUS), in collaboration with HDB, which found that shared facilities, such as linkways, playgrounds, and fitness corners, create opportunities for neighbours to meet and bond.

Centred on the element of co-creation, the project engaged over 1,000 residents and relevant stakeholders intensively through several rounds of pop-up sessions, focus group discussions, interviews,

Members of the community with Minister for National Development Mr Desmond Lee celebrating National Day 2020 at the Community Plaza of Kampung Admiralty.

and design workshops. This resulted in a social linkway with four segments – green link, play link, learning link, and art link, each with its own unique characteristics – that were clusters for different activities and brought resident groups together for greater interaction opportunities. Today, the spaces register about 200 unique visitors daily, where one in three interact with their neighbours.

Since then, HDB has successfully piloted several co-creation projects with residents, from building the first community-designed playground to engaging residents on new facilities for replacement sites under the Selective En bloc Redevelopment Scheme (SERS), as well as garnering ideas for social nodes at towns slated for rejuvenation under ROH 3.

In 2016, HDB launched its Friendly Faces, Lively Places (FFLP) Fund, now renamed as the Lively Places Programme, to inspire residents to initiate and implement ground-up projects that pave the way for active and cohesive communities. As of December 2019, HDB has received over 250 applications that generated over 60,000 volunteering hours from the community.

HDB also introduced its Build-a-thon innovation challenge, now known as the Lively Places Challenge, which also provides design-thinking workshops for all participants to be better equipped with the engagement tools to develop and implement their ideas. As of December 2019, HDB has trained more than 300 participants, who have gone on to helm 67 community projects.

BUILD-A-PLAYGROUND

Designed and built by residents

Mr Markus Koo, Chairman of Canberra Zone 1 Residents' Committee, helped rally community efforts behind the Adventure Playground @ Canberra.

AS a gentle breeze blows, the warm rays of the late afternoon sun fall on a treehouse structure, casting dancing shadows onto the playground in Sembawang Close.

Under the green canopy, children clamber up climbing structures and hammocks that resemble fishing nets, shouting and laughing as they embark on their '*kelong* adventures' (*kelong* is Malay for wooden offshore platforms that are typically used for fishing). Parents chatter away with their neighbours by the benches, as they keep an eye on their little ones.

Welcome to The Adventure Playground @ Canberra – Singapore's first community-built playground.

From conceptualisation to design and assembly, the 185 sq m playground – around the size of two 4-room flats – was created from scratch by some 1,800 residents living in the Canberra housing estate. This came under HDB's pilot Build-A-Playground initiative.

It pays tribute to Sembawang's heritage, an area once dotted with fishing villages and *kelongs*, or fishing jetties.

HDB had supported the project by organising design workshops and roadshows for the residents, as well as surveys, from the middle of 2015 to 2017.

"The challenge was in engaging residents and making sure they are getting something they want," said Mr Markus Koo, Chairman of Canberra Zone 1 Residents' Committee, who was involved in engagement efforts such as door-to-door visits.

"We also had to pacify a few residents because of the noise from the construction. But it all worked out in the end."

The Adventure Playground @ Canberra was completed in January 2018. **"When I see kids playing at the playground, it makes me proud,"** he said, beaming.

The Build-A-Playground pilot has been extended to five more playgrounds in Toa Payoh, Pasir Ris, Woodlands, and Choa Chu Kang. The hope is for more HDB residents to come together and co-create playgrounds that are meaningful for them.

LIVELY PLACES CHALLENGE (PREVIOUSLY HDB BUILD-A-THON)

A green makeover for HDB spaces

For Mr Leon Yeo, the HDB Build-a-thon, now renamed the Lively Places Challenge, not only sparked an idea for a small community hydroponics farm, but also helped him realise the idea with a funding of up to $20,000.

"I was watching this documentary about how some restaurants in Singapore were growing their own herbs for their dishes, and becoming more self-reliant in terms of food sources," shared the Woodlands Drive 16 resident, who is also a member of the Residents' Committee.

"So I thought, 'Can we do that, given the little land that we have in our housing estate?' The only way to do this was to use hydroponics."

After nearly three months, during which he and his team attended hydroponics farming classes, located a suitable site, cleared the land, and found a vendor for the hydroponics system, the Hydroponics Farm@ Woodlands Glen was up and running.

The humble yet high-tech 30 sq m farm – which takes up the space of half a 3-room HDB flat – is full of greens that are commonly sold in supermarkets, from *cai xin* and *gai lan* (leafy green vegetables often used in Asian cooking), to spinach and lettuce.

"Not many housing estates have a hydroponics farm, so for residents here, it is an opportunity to experience something new. They also get to taste the greens that they harvest themselves," he said.

The farm is also a place for residents to bond. Since opening in March 2019, over 200 residents have participated in the gardening activities and formed firm friendships.

"Each time someone peeks into the farm, they are always invited inside. This is the first step for residents to start a conversation and get to know each other. We want to create a special place where residents can bond," he added.

Besides Mr Yeo's project, the Lively Places Challenge has attracted many other innovations throughout its three editions including Team Konnectorize, which turned the void deck of Block 683C Woodlands Drive 62 into an Instagram-worthy hang-out spot boasting 3D wall murals, floor decals, additional lightings, and a plant wall.

Another group, Sembawang Rangers, revamped the residents' corner at Block 718 Woodlands Avenue 6 to provide residents with a more open and conducive space that they can call their own.

Mr Leon Yeo stands proudly in front of the Woodlands Glen hydroponic farm which his team helped to set up.

CHAMPIONS OF THE HEARTLAND

SHAPING positive and endearing heartland living experiences is perhaps most meaningful and impactful when led by residents themselves.

In 2017, HDB's Friends of Our Heartlands (FOH) network was launched to bring together the wide range of community-building and volunteering programmes under one umbrella. Drawing over 9,700 volunteers, it is a holistic platform that also helps like-minded individuals and organisations tap on partnership opportunities.

The young and youths can join the Heartland Ambassador Programme, specially designed to help students in primary school up to post-secondary levels become champions of gracious and responsible heartland living.

Students from various Institutes of Higher Learning who led primary and secondary students on a door-to-door outreach effort at Tampines Central.

FRIENDS OF OUR HEARTLANDS (FOH) NETWORK

A home away from home

WHEN Singapore Permanent Resident Pradip Mandal first set foot in Singapore with his wife and three-year-old son in 2007, it was the beginning of his love affair with the Lion City.

"It was like love at first sight," said the 45-year-old, who had moved to Singapore for a work opportunity.

"Back then, the amenities in Punggol were basic, but there was a lot of natural beauty around. I realised that Punggol would grow and bloom in future. With that hope, we made Punggol our new home."

A year after he and his wife settled in, they welcomed their second child, a daughter.

Mr Mandal started to become more active in the community in 2014, when he took part in the Good Neighbours Project, now renamed the Lively Places Programme, an initiative that encourages ground-up projects to promote neighbourliness.

In 2018, he joined HDB's FOH volunteer network. **"The FOH volunteer programme is even more special because it relates to HDB living, which my family and I have been enjoying for close to 12 years now,"** he said.

Together with two other FOH volunteers, Mr Mandal facilitated his first engagement session with HDB residents living near Tembusu Park in Choa Chu Kang, gathering residents' input on a new adventure playground to be built in the park.

He has gone on to take part in other events, such as at Punggol Town Square where he played tour guide to a group of seniors on their day out. He also joined the Lively Places Challenge 2020, where participants proposed and implemented innovative solutions to create friendly and lively neighbourhoods.

Started in 2017, the FOH network has drawn over 9,700 volunteers like Mr Mandal, who have given their time and talent to build strong communities in the heartlands.

Despite his busy schedule as an IT project manager, he believes it is important to give back to the community. He volunteered to be a Safe Distancing Ambassador as Singapore battled the COVID-19 outbreak in 2020, encouraging members of the public to adhere to safe distancing measures in HDB estates.

"Living in an HDB estate has been meaningful for me. Our flat in Edgedale Plains has become our home away from home, and my two children have grown up playing with many of their friends in the neighbourhood, in a very safe environment," he said.

For Mr Pradip Mandal (third from left) and his family, Singapore has become home.

INTER-AGENCY COLLABORATION

Working hand in hand

THE idea of collaboration has increasingly underscored community-building efforts, helping to bring them to fruition. While many of these ground-up initiatives are reflective of HDB's collaboration with the community, another side of ensuring a cohesive and vibrant community involves working hand in hand with other government agencies.

For Mr Mike Chan, Deputy Chief Executive Officer (Estate), and his team, it all stemmed from an earlier incident when they visited a flat in Tampines.

Even before they stepped into the home of Mr Lee (not his real name), they were hit with a pungent smell. The stench, they found, as they entered the house, was the smell of urine.

"Mr Lee had been storing his own urine in bottles and it created such a bad smell that the neighbours started to complain," said Mr Chan. **"But who was responsible for helping him? His family members were ignoring him. His wife had left him, and his children were staying on their own, so he was all alone with his bottles of urine and loads of old clothes, *karung guni* (a colloquial term for 'rag-and-bone') items that he insisted were valuable and of great sentimental value to him."**

Various organisations like the National Environment Agency (NEA), the Institute of Mental Health (IMH), the Ministry of Social and Family Development (MSF), Town Councils, and community leaders were roped in to resolve the case.

The Town Council was called in, for instance, so that the contractors could clear the rubbish inside the house and clean the space. IMH or social workers were also required to come in to assess if there were any behavioural issues, while the Singapore Police Force (SPF) and the Singapore Civil Defence Force (SCDF) were on standby in the event of danger.

With the success of such collaboration, the Municipal Services Office (MSO) formalised the Hoarding Management Framework, where a systematic process was put in place for HDB and various agencies to work together to tackle the complexities of hoarding cases in HDB flats in a holistic manner.

"We were able to resolve many cases, with the help of the residents' close relatives," Mr Chan shared. **"So creating active and cohesive communities may not be just for happy things. It can be for anything, whenever someone needs help."**

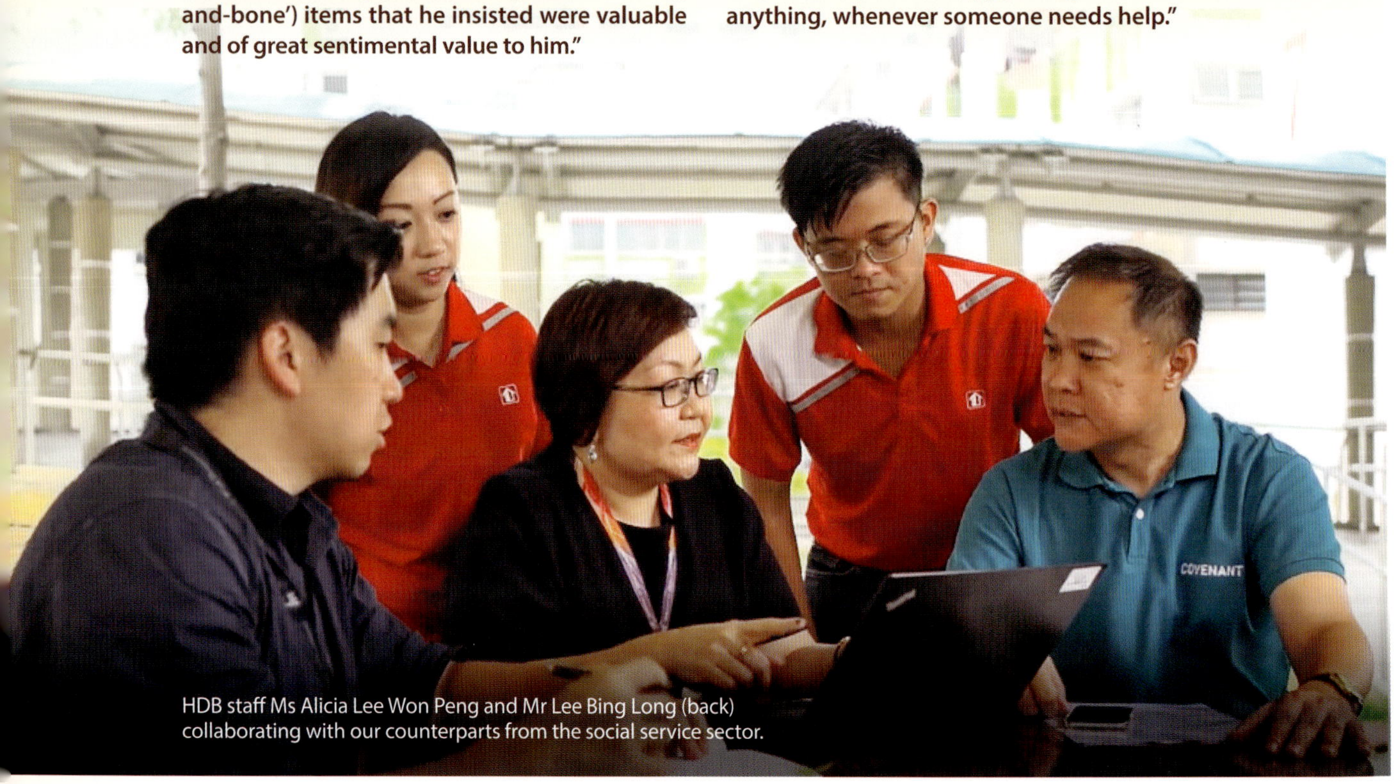

HDB staff Ms Alicia Lee Won Peng and Mr Lee Bing Long (back) collaborating with our counterparts from the social service sector.

Bedok Town Centre

EVOLVING WITH THE TIMES

IN the past 60 years, HDB has provided Singaporeans with more than just a roof over their heads. The public housing agency has given residents a home – a place where family and friends gather, a place for comfort and community.

The work of building homes and creating communities continues. To figure out more approaches in developing the 'new urban *kampung*', HDB collaborated with the Singapore University of Technology and Design (SUTD) and Électricité de France (EDF) to conduct a three-year social behavioural study – the New Urban Kampung research programme.

This in-depth multi-disciplinary study combines the fields of behavioural studies, computational social science, and urban informatics to simulate how the demographics in HDB towns are likely to evolve. Through a combination of Big Data and advanced modelling tools, it also aims to help HDB better understand residents' needs and what they think will make a liveable town.

Insights gleaned will inform strategies that improve environmental and social sustainability, and steer future town planning and housing designs that will enhance the HDB living experience.

Looking ahead, the future for HDB living will be shaped by new and exciting features, as well as continual policy reviews that will create vibrant, cohesive communities.

CHAPTER 5

HOMEWORK

CREATING HOMES THAT WORK

In modern day Singapore, it is easy to take for granted the little joys in life. Most people have comfortable beds to rest in at night, and hot showers to enjoy after a long day at work, with clean water running from the taps.

Yet, life was not always like this, especially not before the Housing and Development Board (HDB) embarked on its task to house a generation of Singaporeans in the 1960s.

Instead, it was more common to find a family of two adults and four children squeezed into one tiny room in a shophouse, with no washroom or kitchen of their own, or a home flooded with muddy water each time it rained, bringing with it unwanted guests such as roaches and rats.

As Singapore developed, blocks of HDB flats – each taller than the last – provided new homes that were much better than the crowded run-down shophouses or *kampungs*.

In the last 60 years, HDB has built self-sufficient, community-centric towns that provide residents with easy access to a range of amenities, such as shops, schools, childcare centres, clinics, playgrounds, and fitness corners. They offer a comfortable, barrier-free living environment for Singaporeans, catering to the needs of people from all demographics and bridging communities.

Today, there are more than one million flats across 24 towns and three estates, occupied by people across all generations. Each home has its own story.

For the elderly couple in their 60s or 70s, their flat is a comfortable retirement home with the ground floor community spaces functioning as spots where they gather with neighbours. For the single woman in her 40s or 50s, home is a quiet sanctuary where she enjoys her hobbies of cooking and baking. For the young couple relishing the experience of being first-time flat owners, their new Build-To-Order (BTO) flat is filled with hopes and aspirations for their future together.

The stories in this chapter tell of Singapore's early struggles and how careful planning laid the solid foundations for the country's progress. They tell of the desires and dedication of residents to forge better lives for themselves and their loved ones, and they put into focus the pivotal role that HDB has played to build good homes and support flourishing communities.

LETTERS TO HOME

Lim Yan Siong, 90

WHEN I BOUGHT MY FIRST HOME...

We still had to make ends meet despite having a home for ourselves. To earn more money, I rented out one room, and squeezed with my wife and four children in the other. In later years, my children's families would always come over for dinner on Saturday evenings, and the flat would be packed with more than 10 people. Today, the old block and Nile Road have all but disappeared, replaced with blocks of newer and taller flats.

THREE THINGS I LOVE ABOUT MY HOME...

It is bigger and much more spacious than my previous home at Nile Road. The location is very convenient, with Tiong Bahru Market and the MRT station just a 10-minute walk away. I now live on the 21st storey, and my unit is well-ventilated and airy. I also get a great view of the harbour from my window, which looks beautiful at night.

LEFT: Mr Lim Yan Siong and his wife attend to their two grandchildren in their old home at Nile Road.

MIDDLE: Mr Lim (in white, by the door) looks on as his wife poses for a photo with their grandson.

RIGHT: Mr Lim (right) and his wife.

In the early 1950s, Shantou-born Lim Yan Siong was one of the many Chinese immigrants who came to Singapore in search of a better life. Home in post-war Singapore then was a single rented room in a derelict shophouse along Coleman Street, where the Grand Park City Hall hotel now stands. Together with his wife and four children, the Lims shared a washroom and kitchen with four other families for almost a decade.

Mr Lim worked numerous odd jobs to make ends meet, which included being an illegal taxi driver and a street vendor. Work finally brought reward when he saved enough to buy a home for his family.

In 1963, he bought his first home – a 3-room flat along Nile Road – for just $6,000. Over the next 39 years, the humble unit on the sixth storey of Block 53 bore witness to three of his children's marriages, and the arrival of four grandchildren.

In 1997, the block was selected for redevelopment under the Selective En bloc Redevelopment Scheme (SERS). With the opportunity to upgrade once more, the Lims moved into a 5-room unit along Kim Tian Road in 2002. The clean, spacious home that Mr Lim lives in today is a far cry from the cramped conditions he first experienced as a young man.

ON WEEKENDS, MY HOME IS...

Packed with my grandchildren who come for dinner on Saturday evenings. We will set up a bigger table to fit everyone. My wife and I will spend the entire day cooking up a feast. After dinner, everyone will gather around the television for fruits and dessert. Saturday is always my favourite day of the week.

LETTERS TO HOME

G Thilagarani, 56

Madam G Thilagarani, 56, has moved homes at least four times in her life to accommodate her growing family. But each location holds a special place in her heart.

It all began in 1987 when she and her husband settled into a 4-room flat in Potong Pasir as newlyweds. They had their first son a year later.

As she was expecting her second son, the couple moved into a more spacious flat in Clementi. The 5-room unit became the family home for the next 10 years, where they welcomed their third son. There, Madam Rani's three sons built forts out of mattresses and played catch at the old railway tracks at Sunset Way, just below their unit.

This was also where she met one of her closest friends, Ms Wong Jee Foon, a mother of two boys herself. Madam Rani and Ms Wong found that they had plenty in common, and both women would often confide in each other about family, work, and motherhood issues over tea in their living rooms.

When Madam Rani's first son got married in 2018, Ms Wong even assumed the role of the groom's godmother to assist in matrimonial proceedings. The two friends still catch up with each other at least once a month.

As the boys got older, the family moved again in 1999 – this time to a 5-room unit in Jurong West.

Today, the family remains tight-knit, with the siblings often gathering at their eldest brother's house in Serangoon and watching football matches together.

As someone who has always treasured relationships, Madam Rani now plays an important role in her neighbourhood as a Resident's Network Manager, where she organises community outreach programmes to empower residents and forge lasting friendships across the estate.

THE HOME I GREW UP IN WAS...

A 5-room Bukit Gombak flat I shared with my parents and seven siblings. We shared rooms and there was never really a time you could be alone, but there was a beauty in growing up in a big family. Everyone pitched in. The large kitchen was a place all of us converged to help cook. Sundays were always memorable because my mother would cook up a storm for the family as a treat for us getting through a hectic week.

WHEN I BOUGHT MY FIRST HOME...

There wasn't any time to feel nervous or afraid of what was to come. We had just gotten married and our first son was about to be born. But we knew it was the start of something new. Having a place we could call our own was a way of creating a new world for ourselves, just as our parents had done before us.

ON WEEKEND MORNINGS...

I am up by 5am to jog at a nearby park with my husband. We will then shop for groceries and buy breakfast for our sons. The family will have breakfast together – a time that I always treasure, as my sons are all grown up. I'll ask them about their week and they will share with me everything that is happening in their lives.

RIGHT: Madam G Thilagarani and her husband (couple from right) with their first son in her parents' home in Bukit Gombak.

BOTTOM: The couple and their three boys when their eldest son got married.

LETTERS TO HOME

Chan Wai Lin, 61

For Ms Chan Wai Lin, 1994 was a year to remember. It was when she had finally found a cosy home she could call her own.

The 3-room HDB flat in Clementi, which she bought under the Single Singapore Citizen Scheme at 35 years old, had met all of her requirements: a good location, reasonable price, and a quiet neighbourhood.

She has been living there happily for more than 25 years now, accumulating many treasured memories.

Even though she is retired, Ms Chan is a firm believer in active ageing. Over the years, she has enjoyed hosting friends at her home, where they do all sorts of things together, from singing to cooking and baking.

The ever-hospitable former educator has even printed a brochure for visitors, explaining what her home means to her, how she bought the flat, and what activities they can enjoy doing there.

She also counts her blessings for being able to live near her siblings and her maternal home, a 5-room flat in Farrer Road.

TOP: Ms Chan Wai Lin (middle) with her siblings inside their Farrer Road flat in 1991.

FAR RIGHT: The brochure Ms Chan made for her home.

RIGHT: Ms Chan (second from left) with her sisters in 2018.

HOME TO ME MEANS...

A haven of rest and refreshment for the spirit, as well as a place for fellowship and to extend hospitality to family and friends.

THREE THINGS I LOVE ABOUT MY HOME:

My home has been a sanctuary for me to rest, relax in, and nurture my hobbies of reading, writing, and practising hospitality. It is a cosy place and is easy to maintain. I like the facilities around my estate, and am able to get around smoothly with the efficient transport system.

IN 10 YEARS, I HOPE MY HOME WILL BE...

A haven outfitted for me to age in place, and a place of respite for family and friends to gather.

LETTERS TO HOME

Vivian De Silva, in her 60s

HOME TO ME MEANS...

More than a roof over my head. It is a sanctuary where I can laugh and cry without being judged.

THREE THINGS I LOVE ABOUT MY HOME:

It is cosy and comfortable. It is where I chill, listen to music, and bake. It is conveniently located in Bedok.

LEFT: Ms Vivian De Silva posing with an illustration of Bedok Beacon, where she has bought a new 2-room Flexi flat.

RIGHT: Ms De Silva is all smiles as she looks forward to a new chapter in her life.

Ms Vivian De Silva has a simple wish: To have a secure nest egg for the rest of her life. That is set to come true for the retiree, who will be selling her 4-room flat to right-size to a new 2-room Flexi flat in a BTO project, with a 35-year lease.

She is looking forward to a new chapter in her life when she moves to her new place, which will be ready by 2022. Besides for retirement, Ms De Silva is also planning to use the extra money for travel, and to continue with her passion as a netball umpire without worrying about finances.

Ms De Silva's new home will be in Bedok Central, just down the road from her current flat. She is glad to be able to remain in familiar surroundings with amenities like banks and the MRT station nearby. Having a smaller flat also means it will be much easier to maintain. **"It's very conducive and comfortable for one person,"** she said.

More importantly, she wants her new home to be a warm space for hosting and entertaining friends and loved ones too – one that will be filled with plenty of joy, laughter, and peace.

IN 10 YEARS, I HOPE MY HOME WILL BE...

A place I'm proud of and secure in.

Chua Lye Huat, 67

One image from the 1950s is still seared in Mr Chua Lye Huat's memory: Sewage water the colour of *teh* (Hokkien for 'milk tea'), with floating critters like rats and cockroaches, had filled the living room of his flat during a particularly bad flooding incident.

Flooding was common in such homes back then, especially during the monsoon season. He had to sleep on the table that night, instead of his usual straw mat on the floor.

But Mr Chua has since seen a dramatic improvement in living conditions from his childhood. Now, he lives in a much bigger 4-room flat, which was recently spruced up under the Home Improvement Programme (HIP). He had chosen to upgrade the unit's ageing bathrooms.

His flat is a five-minute walk from Heartbeat@Bedok, an integrated development where he has been taking ukulele lessons to entertain his grandson who was born in May 2019. He would show off his newly-learnt skills to baby Andrew, who would wave his fists and wriggle his toes in approval.

Mr Chua, who is in his late 60s, also visits the library and polyclinic there.

Having lived in Bedok for more than 30 years, the taxi driver has witnessed the evolution of the area under the Remaking Our Heartland (ROH) programme. Now, he frequents Heartbeat@Bedok and never fails to find time to enjoy his favourite *chwee kueh* (a typical breakfast dish of steamed rice cake served with preserved radish) at the revamped Bedok Interchange Hawker Centre.

WHEN I BOUGHT MY FIRST HOME...

I truly felt the luxury of space in our 4-room flat. We cherished the privacy and enjoyed cooking together in the big kitchen of our matrimonial home, which we bought in 1985.

ON WEEKEND MORNINGS...

My wife and I love to go marketing at Bedok before preparing a sumptuous meal for our family. We also do the housework together and I enjoy tending to my plants.

THE HOME I GREW UP IN WAS...

A one-storey Singapore Improvement Trust flat in Henderson, which has been demolished. Seven of us squeezed into one bedroom. My two sisters occupied a double-decker bed while the rest of us slept on straw mats. The room was separated by plywood from another room which we rented out for $22 a month.

FAR LEFT: Mr Chua Lye Huat entertaining his grandson with a ukulele at home.

LEFT: Mr Chua and his family in their previous flat, also in Bedok, in 1992. They moved into their current flat in 2005.

TOP: Mr Chua and his wife Angeline in their current 4-room flat in 2017, on the day their daughter got married.

LETTERS TO HOME

Amriq Ali, 37

Having grown up in the Eastern part of Singapore, Mr Amriq Ali and his wife Ms Shelby Doshi had always wanted to live in the area they were familiar with, near their families.

But that changed when they saw the unique design of The Pinnacle@Duxton on the HDB website. They fell in love with the project's stunning 50-storey-high towers and central location right next to the business district.

In the end, they opted for a 4-room flat at The Pinnacle@Duxton, and moved in in 2010. As first-time applicants, the couple received the Enhanced CPF Housing Grant (EHG). Their unit on the 42nd storey gives them a panoramic view of Chinatown and beyond – a perk that they cherish.

Even though they have settled comfortably in their new Tanjong Pagar home, Mr Amriq and his wife are still attached to the East. Coincidentally, they used to live in opposite blocks in Chai Chee but never met then. The couple returns to Ms Doshi's old home in Bedok twice a week to visit.

HOME TO ME MEANS...

Happiness, comfort, and warmth.

LEFT: Ms Shelby Doshi in her old Chai Chee flat.

MIDDLE: Mr Amriq Ali in his old Chai Chee flat.

RIGHT: For the young couple, The Pinnacle@Duxton was love at first sight.

THREE THINGS I LOVE ABOUT MY HOME:

We love the unobstructed view of the city from our home and its central location. We also enjoy the amazing view of Singapore from the sky gardens.

IN 10 YEARS, I HOPE MY HOME WILL BE...

Nearer to more attractions with the upcoming Greater Southern Waterfront.

LETTERS TO HOME *Huldah Chin, 28*

As children, Ms Huldah Chin and her husband Mr Joash Chong were used to running around in their spacious homes, flushed with excitement and adrenaline as they embarked on games of their own imagination.

Having lived in a 5-room executive flat and maisonette respectively, the couple naturally wanted ample space for their own marital home.

They opted for a 5-room resale flat in Bukit Panjang, which they moved into in April 2019.

Subsidies offered by HDB opened up a plethora of options, making it easier for them to buy their first home. These included the Proximity Housing Grant (PHG) and the Family Grant, which they qualified for as first-timer applicants.

The couple loves having family and friends over. With both their parents living in the West, such gatherings have become more convenient and in turn, more frequent. Another big boon for them is the flat's location – a short walk to the Bukit Panjang MRT station, where they usually take a 30-minute train ride right into town.

WHEN I BOUGHT MY FIRST HOME...

I relished the sense of freedom and ownership. The freedom to design our own house and have our own rules (or not), alongside the ownership and responsibility in taking care of and maintaining the household. When living under our parents' roofs, we tend not to realise the amount of hard work that goes into ensuring the house is hospitable and comfortable.

BOTTOM: Ms Huldah Chin and her husband Mr Joash Chong in their 5-room flat in Gangsa Road.

TOP RIGHT: Ms Chin (second from right) playing with her three sisters in their 5-room Choa Chu Kang executive flat in 1994.

RIGHT: Ms Chin (far left) and her three sisters in their 5-room Choa Chu Kang executive flat in 1994.

ON WEEKEND MORNINGS...

We watch television, play the football simulator game FIFA on the PlayStation, and sometimes invite our friends over for a few rounds of mahjong.

IN 10 YEARS, I HOPE MY HOME...

Will be a place of refuge and joy for ourselves, our family, and friends.

LETTERS TO HOME

Mohammed Zakaria Bin Zainal Azman, 35

THE HOME I GREW UP IN WAS...

In beautiful Tampines, which received the World Habitat Award for Tampines New Town in 1992. More importantly, it was a home built with the love of my parents. I used to live alone when I was working abroad for short stints of three to six months. It is true that a house is not a home without your loved ones.

WHEN I BOUGHT MY FIRST HOME...

It was magical. The idea of having your own space to build, imagine, and create was something surreal, and the idea of owning your own home meant having a stake in Singapore and being Singaporean. That was empowering considering in many parts of the world, you can only rent.

ON WEEKEND MORNINGS...

We would wake up early to take a walk at Tampines Eco Park that is just 10 minutes away but a total break from city life. It's wild, untouched, and peaceful. A space that allows us to reconnect again with nature. Once back home, I would start to prepare a breakfast of toast, scrambled eggs, and organic coffee. We would then buy groceries for the week ahead at Our Tampines Hub that has pretty much everything we need in one space.

For 34-year-old Mohammed Zakaria Bin Zainal Azman, having a place that he and his wife call home means being able to pursue one of their favourite pastimes – bringing people together through food.

Hosting close friends and family over home-cooked meals has become a big part of the couple's lives since they moved into their 4-room BTO flat in Tampines in 2015.

In fact, their living room has been designed for that very purpose – a cosy communal space and dining area where people can bond over conversations and home-made delicacies.

For Mr Zakaria, having a home in Tampines is also a way for him to reconnect with the past.

Having grown up in a 4-room HDB flat in Tampines with three siblings and his parents, Mr Zakaria holds fond memories of the area, which has evolved over the years. What used to be a barren piece of land near his childhood home, he recalls, is now being occupied by three malls, the Tampines MRT station, and bus interchange.

Residing less than 3 km away from both his parents and in-laws has allowed Mr Zakaria to maintain close ties with his family even after marriage.

From catching up with each other over coffee or going for walks together at the nearby park, Mr Zakaria and his wife continue to build meaningful memories with their parents.

TOP LEFT: Mr Mohammed Zakaria Bin Zainal Azman and his family dig in to a hearty meal.

TOP: Mr Zakaria (right) with his older sister in their childhood home in Tampines.

LEFT: Mr Zakaria and his wife Ms Aqilah in their 4-room BTO flat in Tampines.

The art of customer service

IN my years of working at HDB, I have had the privilege and pleasure of knowing many wonderful colleagues. In particular, I have always admired the patience and dedication of some of our Branch colleagues, who sometimes have to bear the brunt of residents' unhappiness.

A light-hearted moment occurred in 1999, when I was assisting in a Main Upgrading Programme project in the Bukit Merah precinct. Residents were required to poll for or against the project, and towards the last night, there were a few who had yet to vote.

Less than an hour before the polling station closed on the last day, a resident who had already visited the sample unit a few times came down. When the Senior Estate Manager of Bukit Merah Branch Poh Eng Chai (then Principal Technical Officer) asked the resident if she would like to vote for the upgrading package, she said she was convinced of the benefits. However, her husband, a fishmonger, refused to come down to vote after a tiring day at work.

Mr Poh listened patiently, then enquired how she had asked her husband to do so. She said: "I just told him to come down." Mr Poh paused, then suggested that she call him again from the station's telephone to say something along the lines of: "*Qing ai de* ('my dear' in Mandarin), can you come down to vote, please?"

The lady looked a little surprised but took his advice. A few minutes later, a grumpy-looking man (her husband) came to the station, voted, then went back upstairs. In the end, the upgrading programme went ahead very successfully.

This incident was one of several occasions in which I witnessed how Mr Poh handled his duties and the people around him. It convinced me that some of our experienced staff really know how to empathise with and reach out to our residents, because they genuinely understand their concerns, fears, and feelings.

Residents' feedback and consensus are critical to the implementation of various HDB upgrading programmes.

Other Branch colleagues such as Mr Chua Joon Mong (then Branch Head), Mr Wan Cheng Yan (then Senior Estates Manager), and Mr Teo Soo Thye (then Principal Technical Officer), who have since retired, have also impressed me with their tireless dedication.

Till today, I hold the utmost respect for these wonderful colleagues.

Brian Low
Director,
Landscape and Design,
Development & Procurement Group

View from the sky terrace on Level 17 of Alkaff LakeView on 11 January 2020. In the foreground is the realigned Upper Aljunied Road, which opened to the public on 12 March 2017. At centre-left is the detention pond from the infrastructure works, which will double in footprint and be landscaped as it transforms into Alkaff Lake. In the background are BTO projects Woodleigh Glen and Woodleigh Hillside, which are under construction.

Bidadari: Behind the scenes of master planning

IN 2012, as Bidadari's master planning started, I got to know my counterparts from the Research & Planning Group (RPG), the Development & Procurement Group (DPG), the National Parks Board (NParks), and the Public Utilities Board (PUB). We were all relatively young, but we were committed to the vision of making Bidadari an urban oasis filled with nature and heritage. This show of commitment and goodwill made us trust each other readily. Spending nine full days together in master planning charrettes helped speed up the process. Overall, it was a pleasant working experience with a team that possessed strong multi-disciplinary knowledge.

More people have joined the Bidadari team, such as the Project Directors from the Building Quality Group (BQG). It is heartening to know that most of them share the same collaborative ethos, especially those involved in the Bidadari Park project. I believe this team spirit is fundamental to Bidadari's unique master plan and its successful execution. The view of the future Bidadari Park from Alkaff LakeView is breathtaking! (See photo above.)

Over the years, people have also left the Bidadari team for various reasons. It was my turn to leave in August 2019, after almost seven years, as part of my job rotation. Bidadari still occupies a special place in my heart. I wish the current Bidadari team all the best!

Leong Mei Lin
Senior Engineer,
Building & Infrastructure Group

Front-row seat to heartwarming stories

I joined HDB in February 1992 as a Clerical Officer when I was 24 years old.

At first, I found the job tough because I was a quiet and shy person, and I had to face customers every day. I thought of quitting or transferring to a back-end job. But I've had the opportunity to upgrade my service skills over the years. And thanks to good colleagues (*kakis*) and supervisors, and the cheerful working environment, I am still here today. I love my workplace. It is like my second home and together with my colleagues, we are like a big, happy family.

There is one particular incident that I cannot forget. I was working at the selection counter in August 2019 when a divorcee, Madam R., and her teenage daughter came to select a 2-room flat in Sengkang under the BTO exercise. The flat would be ready in 2022. They were accompanied by four other adults and their children. I thought they were relatives, but they turned out to be neighbours.

Madam R. told me that her neighbours had been looking after her daughter while she was at work since they moved into their rental flat in Ang Mo Kio five years ago. They had never expected any payment. The best part is, they were all of different races and religions, yet treated one another like family members.

Madam R.'s neighbours had selected a flat in Sengkang and were encouraging her to apply for a flat in the same town, so they could continue to live close to each other. They also drove her and her daughter to HDB Hub in Toa Payoh to select a flat. They were very excited and helped Madam R. do her homework in choosing her ideal flat. Their story really inspired me. A true friend is one who is always there for you, in good times and in bad. I really respect them.

Offering a host of services at HDB Hub and Branches: Punggol Branch 2013.

I hope HDB will remain for another thousand years or even more. HDB does not just build flats. It builds homes with a lot of love and respect.

Happy 60th anniversary, HDB. Thank you for being a part of my life!

Norsidah Bte Mohamad Nasir
Administrative Executive,
Estate Administration & Property Group

Through the years with HDB

I joined HDB in 1975 as a clerk at the Sales Section, with a starting salary of $200 per month. I have since been attached to a few teams, but my most unforgettable experience was with the Selection Team.

Life at Maxwell Road then was very different. Our Sales Office was in the Annexe block above the canteen at the Ministry of National Development (MND) building. Space was limited, and the wooden tables were shared by two employees each. We sat on wooden chairs and there was no security system in place like today.

Everything was done manually. Preparation lists for selection were hand-copied from the main card system waiting list, and stored by zones and room types. Files for upcoming selections were extracted and bundled according to the dates and times of selection. The cyclostyled selection invitation letters were like forms that we had to fill up by handwriting the required information. We had to be very careful that we copied the correct registration numbers, names, and addresses for each case. Carbon paper was used to duplicate the letters as we needed a copy of each letter.

Flat lists were typed out using manual typewriters, then cyclostyled, collated, and stapled together with selection letters, before they were put into pre-paid envelopes. All sealed letters were then put into the sacks provided by the Singapore Post. Our team members were all very cooperative. We worked together to ensure that all letters were sent on time.

In the 1980s, HDB faced an oversupply of 3-room and 4-room flats. With rising affluence, there was an imbalance in the supply and demand for these two flat types. Our senior officers came up with various ways to reduce the number of unsold flats. For example:

i. We had flats in the Eastern area, where selection was carried out at the Tampines Branch Office. This was to make it convenient for the applicants since most of them lived in the area. At the same time, it also encouraged non-applicants to select a flat when they read about the units on the notice board. Two of our selection officers were attached to the Branch Office to conduct the selection exercise daily.

ii. Orientation tours to Pasir Ris were held bi-monthly to encourage more people to take up the flats in the new town. It was unpopular then as the flats were very far from the city. There were also only a few bus services available and no MRT services. Amenities were limited to neighbourhood shops with the supermarkets and shopping centres still being planned and built at that point in time. The tours created some interest and people gradually took up the flats.

The senior officer in charge of our team then was Mr Tay Koon Quie. He was a fresh graduate, hardworking, and motivated. As the leader, he '*chiong*' (a colloquial term that means 'work hard') all the time and we felt as if we were running in a marathon. Luckily, all of us were in our 20s and had the stamina to keep up with him. He expected us to give our best. He held monthly meetings on how to reduce the unsold flats.

On days when the invitation letters were to be sent out, he waited for us to pack the letters into the sacks, which was often at around 7.45pm, and personally drove the letters to the Singapore Post Mail and Parcel Centre located at Chai Chee Complex.

He wanted to make sure that the applicants would receive the invitation letters on time. At the post office, he had to unload the heavy sacks himself. It was tough but he was not afraid of hard work. He did not just give commands but participated too. He was a true leader who won our utmost respect.

With supportive officers, and cooperative and hardworking staff, we were able to reduce the number of unsold flats and achieve the target set by the management.

As we moved from Maxwell Road to Bukit Merah and then Toa Payoh, we progressed from the manual to the digital era. We experienced many teething problems but managed to overcome them and improve along the way.

Some colleagues have left for greener pastures over the years, but many are still with us. My colleagues and friends whom I have worked with for decades are retiring soon, including me. It has been great working with them.

Happy 60th birthday, HDB. We are all proud to accompany you on a small part of your successful story. Wishing you all the best!

Chew Lay Cheng
Senior Administrative Executive,
Estate Administration & Property Group

THE NEXT CHAPTER: DESIGNING FOR LIFE

EVEN as HDB celebrates its diamond jubilee, its work is far from complete. While the country's biggest housing developer commemorates its achievements in providing affordable, smart and sustainable, and well-designed homes over the past 60 years, it continues to confront new challenges – climate change, an ageing population, maturing infrastructure, diminishing flat leases, and technology disruptions. Cognisant of the changing landscape, Chairman Mr Bobby Chin says:

> "The road ahead will be challenging, but we will keep faith with our mission and deliver quality homes and well-designed towns for the people of Singapore."

This requires an updated strategy and approach, in line with how HDB has continually catered to new aspirations and lifestyles of residents over the years. As HDB enters into its seventh decade, a refreshed roadmap has been drawn up to guide its plans for the next 10 to 15 years. Titled 'Designing for Life', it builds on the existing Roadmap to Better Living in HDB Towns to form three new pillars: **Live Well**, **Live Smart**, and **Live Connected**.

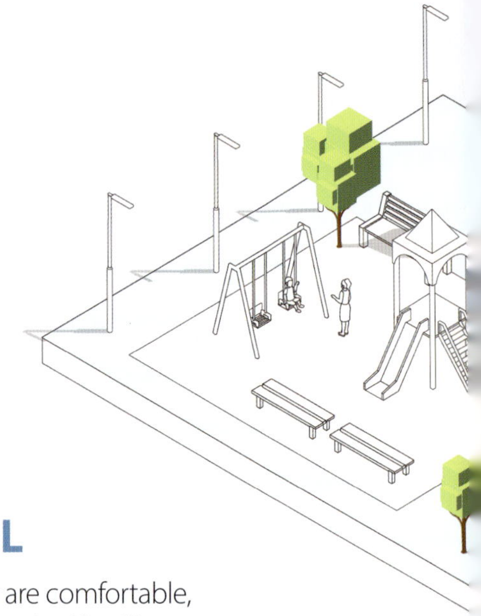

LIVE WELL

HDB towns today are comfortable, visually pleasing, and self-sufficient to ensure that residents can easily access a wide range of amenities and commercial offerings. But there is scope to do more. As aspirations change and more people live longer, HDB will continue to adopt an anticipatory approach to provide for changing lifestyles and the different life stages of residents.

In essence, HDB wants residents to live well. But how can it be achieved? A key strategy is to place greater emphasis on the health and well-being of residents. Under a new Well-being Framework, HDB will formulate strategies to shape and design the built environment to support positive health and well-being outcomes, encourage active lifestyles, foster bonds across all generations, and provide conducive spaces for peace and quiet.

This means having a good mix of commercial, recreational, and healthcare facilities, as well as providing safe exercise equipment and healthy food options. Apart from building physical infrastructure, the small things matter too – even down to how staircases are designed. Imagine having 'statement staircases' that will encourage residents to use the stairs instead of the lift, or even incorporate stair climbing in their daily exercise routines.

Health and Well-Being Planned and Designed into Towns

- New framework to enhance health and well-being in towns
- Residents will be able to maintain good health and forge stronger social bonds

Homes for Different Life Stages and Needs

- Affordable and accessible homes, ease of upgrading and right-sizing, and peace of mind to age in place
- An array of flat layouts and thoughtful detailing that can be customised to suit one's lifestyle

Nature at Our Doorstep

- Biophilic Town Framework to enhance existing natural assets, promote health and well-being, and sustain the ecosystem services
- Opportunities for residents to reconnect with nature and enjoy its intrinsic benefits

Renewing Our Towns for All Generations

- Town-wide rejuvenation – Remaking Our Heartland
- Localised upgrading – Neighbourhood Renewal Programme, Home Improvement Programme
- Long-term replanning and redevelopment – Voluntary Early Redevelopment Scheme

Convenient Access for All

- Well-connected towns that are easily accessible with multiple modes of transport, enhanced with new technology such as autonomous vehicles
- Pleasant, welcoming, and safe streets that encourage active mobility and a healthy lifestyle

A Great Living Environment

- New areas where high-rise living is balanced with comprehensive facilities to ensure liveability
- Innovative planning to ensure adequate space for various needs and stakeholders

Design touches like grab bars offer greater ease and safety at home.

Staircases, often thought of as plain and functional structures, will be embellished with interesting designs and etched with words of encouragement to entice people to use them. These words will include information such as calories burnt and the health benefits gained by climbing stairs. Aesthetics, functionality, and health benefits are all combined into a single stairwell.

"We can be very conscious about health and well-being in the way we design towns," said Chief Executive Officer, Dr Cheong Koon Hean. **"We can design towns such that people can jog around their development precincts, or carry out relaxing activities, such as yoga, amidst serene landscaped spaces."**

A more inclusive environment that caters to all ages and abilities will be developed. These efforts extend to the seniors too. To encourage elderly citizens to stay active and involved in their communities, HDB is designing signage with universally understood pictorial symbols, as well as painting grab bars in contrasting colours to walls. These design touches will help residents navigate their surroundings with ease and confidence.

Beyond physical health, HDB is also exploring ways to improve residents' mental and social well-being through programmes that build bonds and reduce social isolation. This can be done by co-locating facilities such as childcare centres and eldercare centres, and creating partnership programmes to nurture inter-generational bonding.

At the same time, the public space has to be sufficiently diverse with areas for play, exercise, and relaxation to suit the needs of everyone. Within each precinct, HDB will carve out quiet areas that promote restfulness and calmness, where residents can retreat to for peace and mental repose.

All this does not happen by chance, but with careful planning backed by science and data. HDB intends to collaborate with medical and sports experts and agencies such as the Ministry of Health (MOH), Sport Singapore, the Health Promotion Board (HPB), and the Agency for Integrated Care (AIC) to develop the best design for better living.

Artist's impression of pocket garden with seats and landscaping (Residents' courtyard at Bidadari Alkaff Courtview).

LIVE SMART

THE world today is inter-connected, high-tech, and smart. Technology has changed how people live their lives, as smart apps complement and support lifestyles and livelihoods. By using smart technology, HDB aspires to help residents lead more convenient and easier lives.

Living smart is as simple as having homes where residents can easily control their appliances in real time, from anywhere. This will help them better manage their electricity and water usage, and be more mindful of how they consume such resources. Smart tracking and monitoring apps can also be used to help caregivers take better care of seniors who are alone at home, and give them greater peace of mind. Smart-enabled homes also facilitate work and study from home, and open up possibilities to services like tele-medicine.

But HDB is not confining smart-enabled solutions to within homes. In the works are plans to conduct research studies and develop cutting-edge urban solutions, such as centralised cooling, automated waste collection, and environmental sensors, to create efficient, sustainable, and comfortable environments for residents.

By collecting and analysing data, HDB will use the information to optimise estate maintenance, troubleshoot, and pre-empt problems to ensure minimal disruption to estate services. With the data, residents can also be more aware of their consumption patterns and waste levels, and hopefully take steps towards a more sustainable lifestyle.

Intelligent Homes

- Smart-enabled homes allow residents to access services like healthcare in the comfort of their homes, and easily manage their home appliances in real time, from anywhere
- A smart elderly monitoring and alert system can help alert caregivers and family members quickly in times of need, for greater peace of mind

Green, Resource-Efficient Estates

- Technologies, such as smart lighting, solar panels, urban water harvesting, and centralised cooling, make estates more liveable, efficient, sustainable, and safe
- Smart grid allows residents to monitor their energy consumption patterns to reduce energy usage and live more sustainably

Urban Solutions for Greater Comfort and Convenience

- Environmental modelling, noise mitigation strategies, automated waste collection, a network of environmental sensors, and other innovations help create an environment that is more pleasant and comfortable to live in

Seamless and Reliable Services

- To improve estate services, data analytics will be used to optimise maintenance cycles and pre-empt problems for minimal disruption to services
- HDB's Smart Hub serves as the 'brain' for HDB estate operations, collecting and integrating multiple sources of information (e.g. real-time data on energy used by common services), and providing insights to help Town Councils improve estate management

LIVE CONNECTED

BEYOND providing well-designed towns and neighbourhoods, HDB has been playing an active role in connecting communities by developing community-focused initiatives to strengthen community bonds. To continue these efforts, HDB will carry out deeper and more sustained conversations with residents and stakeholders on the planning and design of their towns, including the kind of public spaces and facilities they would like to have in their neighbourhoods.

Today, this is being done through its five-yearly HDB Sample Household Survey (SHS), which is an example of a way to connect with residents and listen to feedback on the ground. Apart from questions on the residents' socio-demographic profiles and their satisfaction levels with HDB facilities, the survey also polls residents on their lifestyles, such as whether they shop online, and the unique places in their towns that hold special memories for them.

But HDB is going one step further by leveraging digital innovations. HDB has conceived the Pulse of the Heartlands initiative – a digital data platform with Artificial Intelligence services that will enable the private sector, start-ups, and individuals to develop an ecosystem of applications and services to better serve the needs of the community. This was done in partnership with the Info-comm Media Development Authority (IMDA) and tech start-up Sentient.io.

In the works is a mobile app to provide residents with a digital directory of the services, amenities, and events in their neighbourhood. Residents will be able to search for dining options and even make appointments with banks and clinics via the app. As residents use these apps, HDB can tap on the usage insights to sense the 'pulse of the heartlands' and improve the effectiveness and design of its programmes to benefit residents.

Making Places and Memories Together

- Reaching out to stakeholders beyond the traditional segments, such as students from tertiary institutions, to research and propose new ideas
- Ramping up opportunities for the community to co-create and co-design proposals, and activate spaces as part of SG Together
- Empowering residents to implement ground-up projects by providing training and seed funding

Nurturing the *Kampung* Spirit

- Leveraging smart apps and data to strengthen awareness of happenings in the neighbourhood, allow for participatory planning, and encourage social interaction
- Using a socio-technical approach to gain better insights and plan for more liveable community-centric housing

Our Town, Our Living Room

- A variety of community spaces and facilities in towns to serve as an extension of our living room, where there are opportunities to bond, interact, and meet neighbours
- Programmes with the community in focus, to generate greater community vibrancy

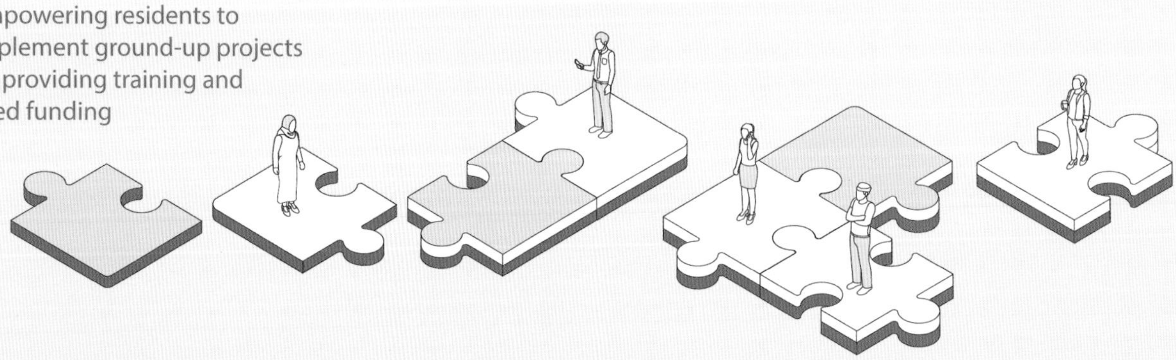

With this understanding, HDB can better devise community enabling tools and design strategies to foster stronger community bonds, empower members of communities to look out for one another, and live connected.

HDB is exploring new ways to empower residents to lead and champion initiatives in their neighbourhoods too. Various capability-building workshops will be organised, and seed funding provided, to better equip residents to lead ground-up initiatives. All this is aimed at increasing their sense of ownership and attachment to their communities, and allowing them to feel at home – even beyond the four walls of their flats.

While programmes and policies have evolved, one thing that has stayed constant at HDB is its focus on people.

Today, with data and technology, HDB is able to take on a more evidence-based approach in its planning and design of towns, policy formulation, and delivery of programmes and services. These new initiatives and ideas require a deep understanding of people, how they live, and the factors that drive behaviour.

Looking ahead, the future for HDB living will be shaped by new and exciting features, as well as continual policy updates that will create vibrant, cohesive communities.

"HDB is in the people business," said CEO Dr Cheong Koon Hean. **"You cannot build towns and homes without understanding people. Because what we deliver is not just a house, but a total living experience. We are designing for life, not just for living."**

HDB's Health and Wellness team. L-R: Ms Phua Shi Hui, Ms Chau Hai Qing, Ms Tang Mei Hwang, Group Director (Research & Planning) Dr Chong Fook Loong, Ms Kathleen Goh, Ms Kwek Feng Yi, Ms Victoria Sng.

Sixty Years

of HDB

HOUSING A NATION: THE FIRST 50 YEARS

A DECADE OF TRANSFORMATION: 2011 TO 2020

HOUSING A NATION: THE FIRST 50 YEARS

1950s

Squatter colonies and ramshackle huts are a common sight across Singapore. Housing shortage is a severe problem.

1960

The Housing and Development Board (HDB) is formed on 1 February 1960 with a clear mandate to solve Singapore's housing crisis, provide affordable housing, and supervise the clearing of slums and carry out urban development. Its main office is set up in Princess House at Queenstown.

The Government unveils HDB's first Five-Year Building Programme to provide 52,842 flats at an estimated cost of \$230 million. The first project, costing \$34 million, provided 10,000 flats to house 60,000 residents.

1961

HDB steps up its construction of 1-room rental flats to rehome 16,000 people affected by a massive fire at the Bukit Ho Swee estate.

1964

HDB carries out its first land reclamation project at Kallang Basin, a six-year project that would conclude in 1969. A total of 199 ha of land would be reclaimed.

HDB, which previously built only rental flats, launches the Home Ownership for the People Scheme. The monthly household income ceiling is set at \$800, and individual monthly income ceiling at \$500. To keep pace with rising wages, the income ceiling would be gradually raised.

Toa Payoh Town,

the **first self-sufficient satellite town**
with access to amenities like schools, shops, clinics, and parks

HDB takes on the role of a mortgage financier, providing flat buyers with housing loans.

HDB develops Toa Payoh Town – the first self-sufficient satellite town with access to amenities like schools, shops, clinics, and parks.

1965

HDB completes its first Five-Year Building Programme.

1966

Tenants move into the first block of flats in Toa Payoh Town. The tenants rent 840 1-room flats in four blocks at a monthly rental of $30. In October, the first 720 flats would be sold to the first flat owners in Toa Payoh.

Land reclamation works begin at Marine Parade.

1968

The Central Provident Fund (Amendment) Act is passed. Citizens can now use a part of their Central Provident Fund (CPF) savings to pay for the down payment and monthly instalments when purchasing a flat.

HDB conducts its first Sample Household Survey (SHS), a large-scale survey done every five years that covers various aspects of HDB living. The survey findings would help fine-tune HDB's policies and improve the HDB living environment. The 2018 SHS is the 11th survey in the series.

1969

HDB completes its first 100,000 units.

1970

HDB moves into its new home at the Ministry of National Development (MND) Building at Maxwell Road.

1971

Flat owners who purchased flats under the Home Ownership for the People Scheme are now allowed to sell them in the open market, after a three-year minimum occupation period, to those on HDB's register of intending purchasers. Previously, they had to sell the units back to HDB.

HDB introduces its first batch of 5-room flats at Kallang Basin. Previously, it built only 1- to 4-room flats.

1972

HDB begins building its first housing estate on reclaimed land at Marine Parade.

1974

HDB and the Urban Redevelopment Authority (URA) set up the Housing and Urban Development Company (HUDC) to provide housing options for middle-income groups.

from **1960** to **1969,** HDB completes its

first 100,000 units

1979

HDB introduces the resale levy concept. Flat owners who have occupied their flats for at least five years will now be allowed to sell their flats at market prices without being debarred from applying for another HDB flat for 30 months – if they pay a transfer fee based on 5 percent of their flat's resale price.

1982

HDB introduces the Multi-Tier Family Housing Scheme, giving priority in housing allocation to multi-generation families intending to live under the same roof.

Flat owners who sell their subsidised flats on the open market now have to pay a graded resale levy ranging from 10 to 20 percent, depending on their flat types. This is regardless of whether they buy another subsidised flat from HDB.

1984

The precinct concept – a scaled down level from the neighbourhood concept – is introduced to provide a more conducive setting for social interaction among residents. The first 'precinct' at Tampines Town is completed.

1985

HDB launches 'Housing a Nation: 25 Years of Public Housing in Singapore' – a publication chronicling the first 25 years of public housing.

HDB revises its resale levy policy. Those selling their subsidised flats can choose to pay either a graded resale levy based on their flat type at the point of sale, or a 10 percent premium (later revised to 20 percent in 1994) on the price of their next subsidised flat at the point of purchase. Those who do not intend to buy another flat from HDB need not pay any levy.

by **1989,**

88%

of Singapore's population of 2.7 million people are living in HDB flats

1986

The interest rate for the HDB concessionary loan is changed from a fixed rate to a floating rate, pegged at 0.1 percent above the prevailing CPF Ordinary Account interest rate.

1987

HDB shifts its headquarters from Maxwell Road to the new HDB Centre at Bukit Merah Central. The move will streamline HDB's operations and house its expanding team of staff.

1988

Town Councils are formed under the Town Councils Act to manage and maintain the common property in public housing estates.

1989

The Ethnic Integration Policy (EIP) is implemented to encourage racial integration and prevent racial enclaves. Quotas are set on the ethnic groups at the block and neighbourhood levels across all HDB estates.

HDB allows Singapore Permanent Resident (SPR) households and private property owners to buy and own resale HDB flats. They are allowed to obtain a market interest rate loan from HDB.

About 88 percent of Singapore's population of 2.7 million people are living in HDB flats.

1990

HDB introduces lifts on every floor for all new public housing blocks.

Marine Parade,

the first housing estate built on reclaimed land

1991

The Design-and-Build Scheme is launched, with HDB calling a tender for the first project at Tampines Street 45.

HDB introduces the Single Singapore Citizen Scheme (SSCS). Single Singaporeans aged 35 and above can buy 3-room or smaller resale flats in any new town or estate, except for those located in or near the Central area. This rule would later be relaxed in 2001 to allow for purchase in any location. By 2004, single Singaporeans could purchase any flat type.

1992

HDB's Main Upgrading Programme (MUP) formally begins after a pilot phase, where eligible estates are rejuvenated over 20 years.

HDB receives the World Habitat Award for Tampines Town. The prestigious award recognises innovative and outstanding housing ideas and projects across the world.

1993

HDB launches the Interim Upgrading Programme (IUP) for younger estates ineligible for MUP. It includes the sprucing up of lift lobbies and construction of covered walkways.

To be more closely aligned with market practices, HDB provides resale flat buyers with mortgage loans of up to 80 percent of the flat value. It grants loans based on the flat's market valuation or its declared resale price – whichever is lower.

1994

The first standalone Neighbourhood Centre, Keat Hong Shopping Centre, in Choa Chu Kang is completed.

HDB introduces the CPF Housing Grant Scheme to help first-timer couples buy resale HDB flats to live with, or near their parents or married child, by giving them a grant of $30,000. The scheme would be revised to a two-tier grant system in 1995 – a lower tier to buy a resale flat in any location, and a higher tier to buy a unit to live with or near their parents or married child.

1995

HDB introduces the Selective En bloc Redevelopment Scheme (SERS) to rejuvenate older HDB estates. Flat owners affected are given the opportunity to move to new flats. The first site announced for SERS comprised 16 four-storey blocks at Boon Tiong Road / Tiong Bahru Road.

HDB announces the privatisation of HUDC estates to allow residents to enjoy the status and privilege of private residential property owners.

HDB introduces the Executive Condominium (EC) Housing Scheme for young Singaporean professionals or graduate married couples who aspire to own private housing but need some help to do so. Developed and sold by property developers, EC units come with initial eligibility and ownership restrictions similar to those of HDB flats. All restrictions are lifted 10 years after the EC developments obtain the Temporary Occupation Permit.

HDB announces the Estate Renewal Strategy (ERS), aimed at revitalising older HDB estates and providing residents with modern amenities. The strategy is a consolidation of on-going estate upgrading programmes, such as the MUP and the IUP.

1996

Prime Minister (PM) Goh Chok Tong announces the blueprint for Punggol 21 that would transform the area into a modern waterfront town of the 21st Century.

1997

HDB allows online submission of resale applications and valuation requests by listed property agents. Full electronic submission of resale applications would be implemented in 2011.

HDB abolishes the option for flat owners to pay a premium on their new HDB flats in lieu of a levy, while increasing the graded resale levy ranging from 15 to 25 percent. Sellers are allowed to defer the payment of the levy with interest until they buy their second subsidised flat.

To encourage financial prudence and be more closely aligned with market practices, HDB introduces credit assessment before granting mortgage loans, and limits buyers to a maximum of two HDB concessionary housing loans. Tenure is capped at 30 years with an age ceiling of 65 years. The Mortgage Servicing Ratio is capped at 40 percent of the household income. A market interest rate is charged to borrowers who are high-income earners or private property owners.

HDB launches the Studio Apartment (SA) Scheme, providing an additional form of housing to meet the needs of the elderly. The units would be equipped with elderly-friendly features.

1998

The CPF Housing Grant is extended to help single citizens buy a resale flat under the SSCS. To encourage singles to take care of their elderly parents, a higher-tier Singles Grant would be introduced in 2008 for those buying a resale flat with their parents.

1999

HDB moves from slab blocks to hybrid blocks with non-corridor facing flats.

HDB completes the first roof gardens on top of multi-storey car parks.

Punggol 21,

a modern waterfront town of the 21st Century

2000

In celebration of its 40th anniversary, HDB publishes 'Toa Payoh – Our Kind of Neighbourhood' – a book documenting the evolution of the first self-sufficient satellite town.

2001

HDB introduces the Lift Upgrading Programme (LUP) to provide lift access on every floor of older flats. The programme accelerates lift upgrading works by delinking it from the MUP and IUP.

HDB pilots the Build-To-Order (BTO) System in Sengkang and Sembawang. The system offers applicants greater flexibility in choosing the location, flat type, and timing of their purchase. Tender for construction of the project will proceed once 70 percent of flats have been booked.

2002

HDB combines the LUP and IUP to become IUP Plus. Both lift upgrading and interim improvement works can now be carried out at the same time.

New building projects are now launched under the BTO System, after HDB suspended the Registration for Flat System.

HDB moves its head office from Bukit Merah Central to HDB Hub at Toa Payoh Town Centre.

the first flats launched under the BTO System were located in

Sembawang & Sengkang

2003

Banks and financial institutions licensed by the Monetary Authority of Singapore (MAS) are now allowed to provide housing loans to HDB flat buyers. HDB stops providing market-rate mortgage loans.

HDB corporatises its Building and Development Division as HDB Corporation, or HDBCorp, to export Singapore's expertise in urbanisation to other countries. HDBCorp would later be acquired by Temasek Holdings and rebranded as Surbana Corporation.

HDB introduces 3-Generation (3G) playgrounds. Children's playgrounds, and adult and elderly fitness corners are combined for the whole family to stay active together.

HDB implements full Electronic Parking System (EPS) at two car parks as part of a pilot project.

2005

HDB introduces the Design, Build and Sell Scheme (DBSS), engaging private developers to construct public housing. The developer will be given design flexibility, while preserving the character of public housing. The scheme would be suspended in 2012.

The maximum Loan-To-Value (LTV) limit for HDB housing loans is raised from 80 percent to 90 percent.

2006

In place of the graded percentage resale levy, HDB revises the resale levy to a fixed amount, ranging from $15,000 to $55,000 – pegged to the flat type of the first subsidised flat. This gives second-timers certainty on the levy amount they have to pay, facilitating their decision-making in buying a second subsidised flat.

HDB introduces the Additional CPF Housing Grant (AHG) to help low-income citizens own their first homes. The income ceiling is set at $3,000. Applicants can receive up to $20,000 in grants, based on their income levels. The AHG would be enhanced in 2007 and 2009, with the income ceiling raised to $4,000 and then $5,000. The maximum grant amount would be raised to $30,000, and then $40,000.

HDB incorporates Universal Design (UD) features into all new public housing projects, enabling a user-friendly environment for residents of all ages and abilities, in particular Singapore's ageing population.

HDB begins organising Welcome Parties for new flat owners to mingle with their future neighbours, and familiarise them with their new living environment.

HDB's first eco-precinct,
Treelodge@Punggol

2007

HDB unveils plans for its first eco-precinct, Treelodge@ Punggol. Green building technologies would be incorporated in a practical and cost-effective manner to encourage energy conservation, efficient resource consumption, and higher recycling rates.

PM Lee Hsien Loong launches the Remaking Our Heartland (ROH) programme to rejuvenate existing HDB towns and estates. Punggol, Yishun, and Dawson are selected for the inaugural programme.

As part of the ROH programme, PM Lee announces plans for Punggol 21 Plus. The updated plan includes the creation of Punggol Waterway, a 4.2 km man-made channel to link Serangoon Reservoir with Punggol Reservoir.

To replace MUP, HDB launches the Home Improvement Programme (HIP) to address common maintenance problems of ageing flats. Flats built up to 1986 that have not undergone MUP are eligible for HIP.

HDB introduces the Neighbourhood Renewal Programme (NRP), to replace the IUP Plus. NRP focuses on block and precinct improvements such as new letterboxes and seating area at void decks, as well as covered linkways, upgraded playgrounds, and fitness corners.

HDB announces the Revitalisation of Shops (ROS) scheme, offering assistance to HDB retailers to boost their businesses by co-funding promotional events and the upgrading of common areas. Tenants also get rent-free periods to renovate their shops.

To inculcate financial prudence and forward planning, HDB introduces the HDB Loan Eligibility (HLE) letter. Flat buyers who intend to apply for an HDB concessionary housing loan will first need to apply for an HLE letter before they commit to a flat purchase. The letter reflects the maximum loan amount granted to the buyers, the repayment period, and monthly instalments.

2008

The first Active, Beautiful, Clean (ABC) Waters project in collaboration with the Public Utilities Board (PUB) at Balam Estate is completed. This pilot helped HDB expand the use of natural features, such as rain gardens, to channel and treat rainwater, and encourage water infiltration in other projects, to establish a more naturally resilient landscape.

2009

HDB establishes the Centre of Building Research (CBR) to spearhead research and development efforts for building and environmental sustainability, while harnessing new technologies for future public housing. Prototypes of new technologies are test-bedded at CBR before their implementation in HDB estates.

HDB launches the first Sale of Balance Flats (SBF) exercise. This sales exercise usually offers buyers a wide range of flat types, locations, and prices.

The Pinnacle@Duxton, HDB's first 50-storey development, is completed, along with HDB's first sky garden.

HDB introduces the Lease Buyback Scheme (LBS), allowing elderly flat owners to sell part of their flat's lease back to HDB to supplement their retirement income.

HDB organises the inaugural Good Neighbour Award, which recognises individuals who have shown exemplary acts of care and neighbourliness.

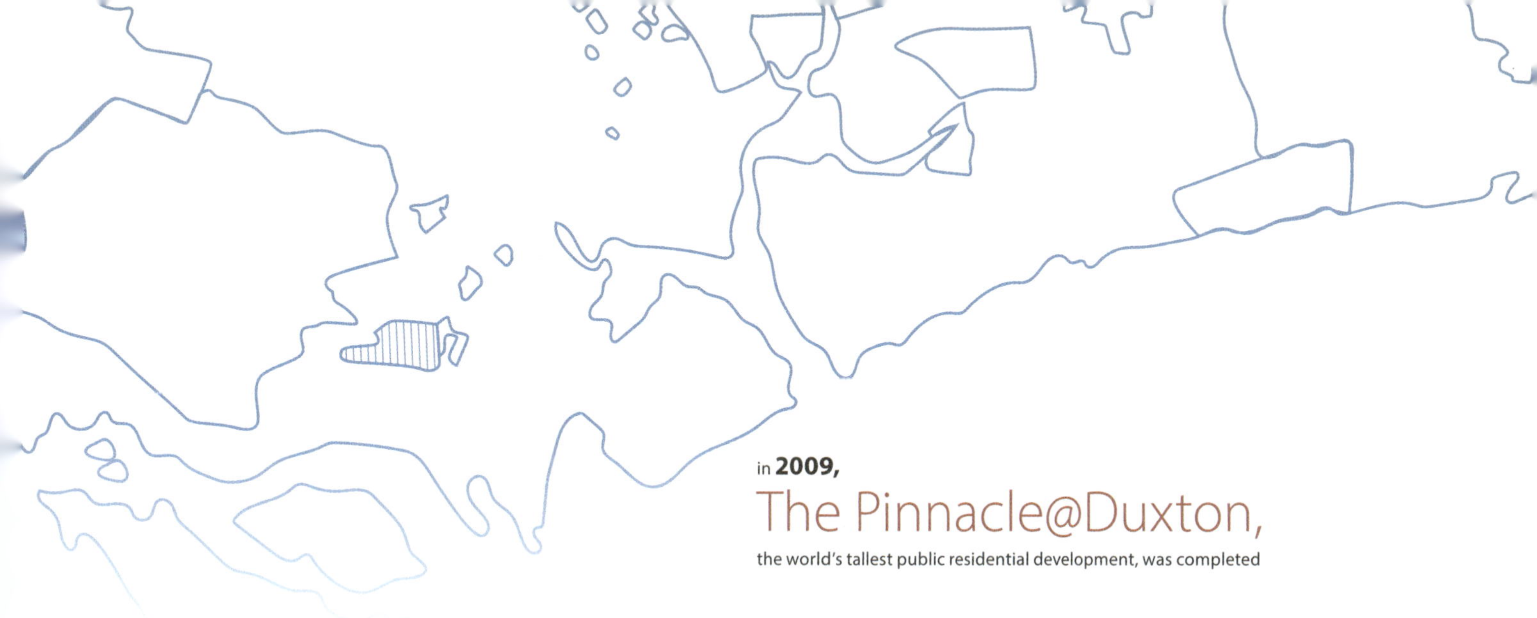

in **2009,**

The Pinnacle@Duxton,

the world's tallest public residential development, was completed

2010

HDB marks its 50th anniversary. As part of its celebration, HDB organises the International Housing Conference in January 2010 and launches its commemorative book '50 Years of Housing a Nation: Our Homes' at a charity gala dinner. In addition, an HDB musical and documentary, both titled 'My Place, My Home', are produced.

Punggol is chosen for development as Singapore's first Eco-Town. The town will serve as HDB's 'living lab' to test-bed urban solutions for sustainable living through effective energy, water, and waste management.

HDB completes its first eco-precinct, Treelodge@Punggol. Treelodge@Punggol is also home to HDB's one millionth flat.

HDB introduces the SPR quota to facilitate better integration of non-Malaysian SPR families into the local community. A limit is set for non-Malaysian SPR families at the neighbourhood and block levels. A non-Malaysian family also has to observe the EIP quota.

To reinforce the principle that HDB flats are meant for long-term owner-occupation, HDB increases the Minimum Occupation Period (MOP) for non-subsidised resale flats from three to five years. Buyers of resale flats are now disallowed from owning both an HDB flat and a private residential property within the MOP.

To widen their housing options, households earning between $8,000 and $10,000 are now allowed to buy new DBSS flats with a $30,000 CPF Housing Grant. Previously, this group was allowed to buy only EC units with the same CPF Housing Grant.

A DECADE OF TRANSFORMATION: 2011 TO 2020

2011

The 4.2 km Punggol Waterway is completed and launched at the Punggol Waterway Fiesta.

East Coast, Hougang, and Jurong Lake areas are announced for the ROH 2 programme. The proposals include the rejuvenation of homes, towns, and neighbourhood centres, improving connectivity to activity nodes and promoting heartland heritage.

HDB unveils its Roadmap to Better Living in HDB Towns – a blueprint to develop towns that are well-designed, smart and sustainable, and community-centric.

HDB develops a Sustainable Development (SD) Framework to guide the development of HDB towns in social, economic, and environmental aspects.

HDB launches the Cool Ideas initiative to co-create solutions for better living with HDB residents.

HDB introduces the Special CPF Housing Grant (SHG), providing low-income families with additional assistance to buy their first flat from HDB. The income ceiling for SHG is $2,250.

The income ceiling for purchase of flats from HDB is raised from $8,000 to $10,000, while that for purchase of EC units from developers is raised from $10,000 to $12,000.

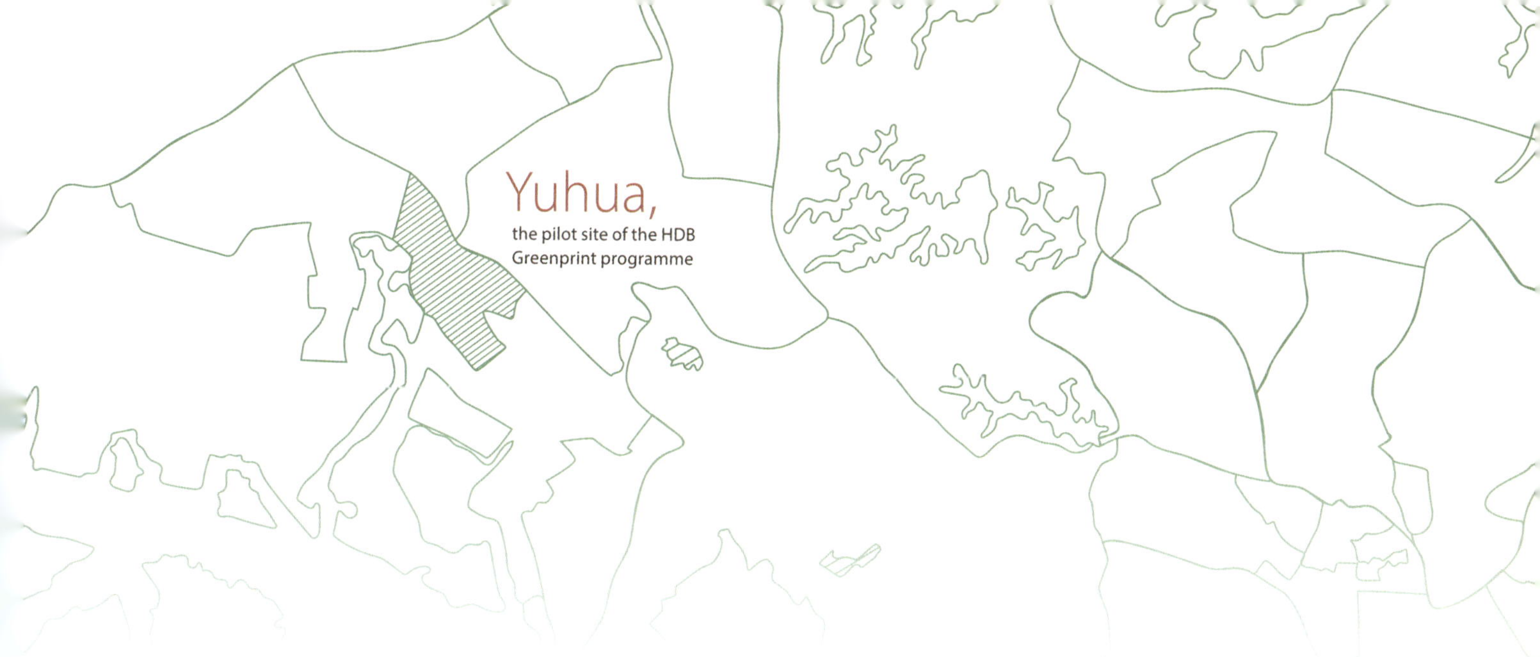

2012

HDB introduces the Multi-Generation Priority Scheme (MGPS) to give priority allocation to married children and their parents who jointly apply for flats to live near each other. Parents must apply for an SA or a 2-room flat, while children can apply for any flat type in the same BTO project.

The first HDB Community Week, an annual event, is held to celebrate the community spirit in the heartlands, and recognise residents' efforts in creating a harmonious living environment.

HDB launches the Enhancement for Active Seniors (EASE) programme to provide elderly-friendly features such as grab bars, slip-resistant treatment to existing bathroom flooring, and ramps in HDB flats.

HDB introduces rooftop gardens on all multi-storey car parks in new public housing developments.

HDB pilots the HDB Greenprint programme in 38 existing HDB blocks at Yuhua. This includes sustainable initiatives in waste management, and energy and water conservation.

2013

HDB introduces the Parenthood Priority Scheme (PPS) to give priority allocation to first-timer married couples with citizen children aged below 16. The scheme would later be expanded to include married couples expecting a child in the same year, and also those with citizen children aged 18 or below in 2019.

To minimise hardship to divorcees and their children, HDB reduces the wait-out period for a divorced couple to each own a subsidised flat from five years to three years. This wait-out period would later be removed in 2018.

HDB enhances the SHG to include middle-income families with a higher income ceiling of $6,500, and first-timers buying new 4-room flats in non-mature estates.

HDB introduces the $15,000 Step-Up CPF Housing Grant to help families living in subsidised 2-room flats in the non-mature estates and public rental flats upgrade to new 3-room flats in non-mature estates.

HDB expands the MGPS to help parents who apply for 3-room flats, in addition to those applying for SAs and 2-room flats.

HDB showcases three new development areas at Bidadari, Tampines North, and Punggol Matilda under the 'Future Homes, Better Lives' exhibition.

First-timer singles aged 35 and above can now buy new 2-room flats in non-mature estates. They can also apply for the AHG (income ceiling of $2,500) and the SHG (income ceiling of $3,250).

HDB launches the Parenthood Provisional Housing Scheme (PPHS) to provide interim housing to married couples as they wait for their BTO flats to be ready.

HDB introduces Three-Generation flats, a new flat type for multi-generation families. These units come with four bedrooms and three bathrooms, two of which are en-suite.

To instil greater financial prudence among flat buyers, the Mortgage Servicing Ratio for HDB housing loans is lowered from 40 percent to 35 percent in January and subsequently to 30 percent in August. The maximum loan tenure is also reduced from 30 years to 25 years.

Rules on the use of CPF savings and HDB housing loans for purchase of flats with a remaining lease of less than 60 years are introduced.

HDB launches the development of a complex system modelling tool with Électricité de France (EDF) and Veolia Environnement Recherche et Innovation. Yuhua estate will serve as the test-bed, simulating various new urban solutions to optimise energy efficiency, effective waste management, water recycling, and transportation networks, among others.

HDB launches the HDB Landscape e-guide, providing consultants with landscape design principles and requirements.

2014

The prototype of the complex system modelling tool for Yuhua estate is officially unveiled at the World Cities Summit.

HDB launches the Cool Ideas Fund, where $500,000 is set aside to encourage inventors to develop ideas to enhance the living environment and test them in HDB towns.

HDB introduces a new resale process where buyers and sellers must agree on the price of the resale flat before seeking a valuation. This removes the need to negotiate the cash-over-valuation – a cash premium that a buyer pays above the valuation of a resale flat.

HDB holds the first edition of the HDB Build-a-thon to empower the community in proposing and implementing solutions to create friendly and lively neighbourhoods. It would later be renamed as the Lively Places Challenge in 2019.

The age criterion for EASE is lowered from 70 years old to 65 years old, benefitting more seniors. Improvement items like grab bars and slip-resistant treatment are now extended to the second bathroom.

HDB enhances the Married Child Priority Scheme (MCPS) that was launched in 2002 to further help married children and parents live with or near each other. Up to 30 percent of the flat supply from BTO and SBF exercises will be set aside for MCPS first-timer families, and up to 15 percent for second-timer families.

HDB introduces a standard suite of eco-features in all new public housing developments such as LED lighting with motion sensor controls to lower energy consumption, as well as centralised chutes for recyclables.

HDB pilots an integrated block with both rental and sold units in Woodlands to allow for better social mixing. This block would be completed in 2018.

HDB launches the Smart HDB Town Framework, mapping out key dimensions that guide the deployment of smart initiatives in its towns and estates.

Punggol Northshore is selected as the first new public housing district to test-bed smart technologies.

Punggol Northshore, the first new public housing district to test-bed smart technologies

2015

Beginning with Tampines GreenRidges, HDB introduces the Pneumatic Waste Conveyance System (PWCS) for housing projects in some of the new towns and estates.

Toa Payoh, Woodlands, and Pasir Ris are announced for the third round of the ROH programme. As it draws up the rejuvenation plans, HDB actively engages residents and stakeholders through focus group discussions.

As part of the SG50 programme, which commemorates the 50th Anniversary of Singapore's independence, HDB launches the SG Heart Map celebration events, culminating in a four-day long finale event held in November 2015.

HDB consolidates demand across multiple government agencies for the installation of solar panels. The tender is called under the government-led solar lead demand programme, SolarNova, which is spearheaded by the Singapore Economic Development Board (EDB).

HDB launches the second test-bedding site for the HDB Greenprint at Teck Ghee to bring green living to more residents.

In line with Singapore's Smart Nation vision, HDB announces some 9,000 Yuhua residents will be the first to experience 'Smart Living' in an existing HDB estate. This builds on the sustainable improvements implemented in Yuhua estate under the HDB Greenprint.

HDB introduces the 2-room Flexi Scheme to better cater to the diverse needs of families, singles, and seniors. The scheme replaces the previous 2-room Scheme and SA Scheme. Seniors aged at least 55 now have the option of buying 2-room Flexi flats on shorter leases, ranging from 15 to 45 years.

HDB raises the income ceiling from $10,000 to $12,000 for the purchase of flats, and from $12,000 to $14,000 for the purchase of EC units.

The SHG is further enhanced, with a higher income ceiling of $8,500 for families, and $4,250 for singles. The maximum grant amounts are also doubled, with families now eligible for up to $40,000, and singles for up to $20,000.

HDB introduces the Proximity Housing Grant (PHG) to encourage families to live with or near each other for mutual care and support. Eligible families can receive a grant of $20,000 when they buy a resale flat to live with, or within 2 km of, or in the same town as their parents or married child. Eligible singles can enjoy a grant of $10,000 if they buy a resale flat to live with their parents.

HDB awards the first SolarNova tender. Under the SolarNova programme, HDB would progressively roll out 220 megawatt-peak (MWp) of solar panels at about 5,500 HDB blocks.

HDB introduces thematic playgrounds. It also enhances greenery in new precincts with more trees, rooftop and vertical greenery.

HDB applies the Biophilic Town Framework in Punggol Northshore District. This framework guides the enhancement of existing natural assets and the development of neighbourhood landscapes that promote a greater sense of place, better health and well-being, and quality of life for residents.

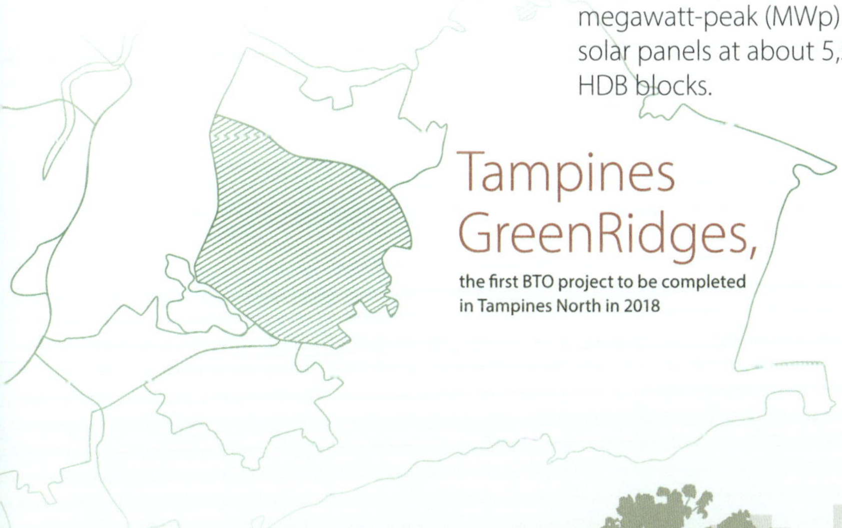

Tampines GreenRidges,

the first BTO project to be completed in Tampines North in 2018

2016

HDB enhances the ROS scheme, increasing the upgrading budget for each shop from \$20,000 to \$35,000.

The HDB Friendly Faces, Lively Places Fund is announced with a funding of \$500,000 over five years for the community's ground-up projects.

HDB reveals the master plan for its 24th town, Tengah, which will feature extensive greenery and elements such as Community Farmways and the Forest Corridor. It will also be the first HDB town planned with smart technologies town-wide from the outset.

The Cool Ideas Fund is enhanced, with \$600,000 set aside for winning participants to transform their prototypes into workable ones for test-bedding in HDB blocks.

HDB launches its first landscape master plan, which will link seven housing projects in Dawson in a series of green spaces and pathways.

HDB introduces the Fresh Start Housing Scheme to help second-timer families with young children living in public rental flats to own a home again.

HDB pilots MyNiceHome Roadshows for new flat owners to familiarise themselves with their new living environment and equip themselves with useful information and tips on HDB living. The roadshows would replace the Welcome Parties, which would later cease in 2019.

Tengah,

the first HDB town planned with smart technologies town-wide from the outset

2017

HDB enhances the CPF Housing Grant to provide eligible resale flat buyers with more housing options. To encourage prudent housing choices, more help is given to those buying smaller flats. The grants for first-timer families buying a 4-room or smaller resale flat are $50,000, and $40,000 if they buy a 5-room or bigger resale flat. First-timer singles receive half of these amounts.

HDB exhibits the ROH 3 plans for Woodlands, Pasir Ris, and Toa Payoh. The plans incorporate suggestions from residents at focus group discussions.

HDB launches the Friends of Our Heartlands (FOH) network, which incorporates all of HDB's volunteering programmes.

HDB launches the biannual Re-Offer of Balance Flats (ROF) exercise. It pools together flats not taken up in previous SBF exercises.

All new public housing blocks will be designed with solar-ready roofs, where feasible. This enables a more productive and efficient installation of solar panels on HDB rooftops.

HDB pilots the Prefabricated Prefinished Volumetric Construction (PPVC) method in a new public housing development at Yishun.

'Smart Community' is added to the Smart HDB Town Framework as a new domain. The objective is to leverage information and communications technologies, and data analytics to better engage residents, enhance community bonding efforts, and empower communities to take greater ownership in co-creating their living environment.

HDB embarks on the New Urban Kampung research programme in collaboration with the Singapore University of Technology and Design (SUTD) to better understand the quality of life in HDB towns, predict demographic changes, and gain insights into residents' needs and responses to their living environment.

HDB announces the Deferred Downpayment Scheme and the Temporary Loan Scheme (TLS) to assist seniors who are right-sizing in deferring the down payment until they collect the keys to their new flat. It also facilitates the transition to their new home before the sale of their existing flat is completed.

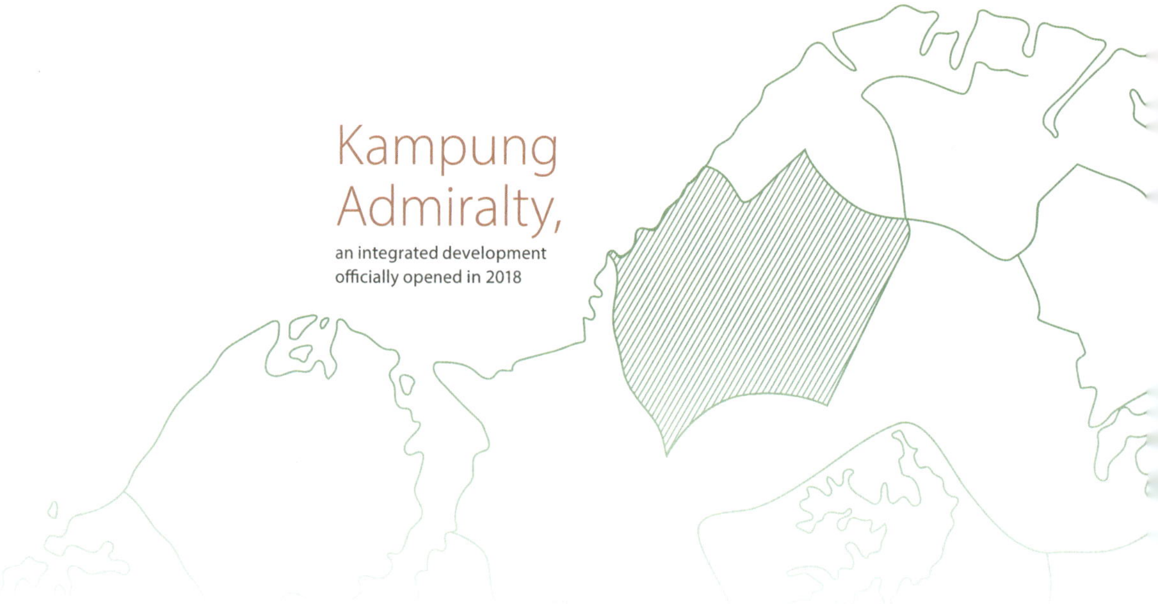

Kampung Admiralty,

an integrated development officially opened in 2018

2018

HDB launches the first batch of flats with shorter waiting time where construction would commence ahead of their launch, to reduce the waiting time for couples buying their first homes.

The first community-built playground under the Build-A-Playground initiative is completed and opened at Canberra, Sembawang.

HDB enhances the PHG and simplifies its criteria to a distance-based condition of 4 km. Eligible families who buy a resale flat to live with their parents or children can enjoy a higher-tier PHG of $30,000, while those living nearby can enjoy a PHG of $20,000. These grants would be halved for eligible singles.

HDB removes the three-year wait-out period imposed on divorcees who wish to buy a subsidised flat, as long as they meet the eligibility conditions for the flat purchase.

HDB launches the book 'Nature, Place & People' at the World Cities Summit, a documentation of the Biophilic Town Framework. The book is a culmination of a three-and-a-half year research project by HDB, URA, National University of Singapore (NUS), and National Parks Board (NParks).

HDB inks an agreement to research the use of 3D concrete printing for the production of unique architectural forms, to expand its design and construction capabilities.

HDB extends HIP to flats built between 1987 and 1997, a move that will benefit about 230,000 households. It also introduces HIP II that will see all flats upgraded a second time when they hit 60 to 70 years.

PM Lee announces the Voluntary Early Redevelopment Scheme (VERS) at the National Day Rally, as part of long-term plans to renew and rebuild older HDB towns when flats are around 70 years or older.

HDB introduces Town Design Guides with the launch of the first guide for Woodlands Town. These guides will serve as references for agencies and Town Councils to enhance the distinctive identity of each HDB town.

An open platform, Cool Ideas Enterprise, is launched, where local start-ups and enterprises will co-develop innovative solutions to address HDB's challenges and improve residents' quality of life.

Ramp solutions, such as portable ramps and customised ramps for flats with multi-step entrances, are offered as part of the EASE package. HDB also implements a wheelchair lifter pilot scheme for homes where ramps cannot be installed.

Kampung Admiralty, Singapore's first 'vertical *kampung*', is officially opened by PM Lee. The integrated development brings together housing units and facilities such as a medical centre, an active ageing hub, and retail outlets under one roof.

2019

HDB completes the implementation of full EPS at 1,841 car parks islandwide – 95 percent of the car parks feasible for EPS.

Three initiatives – the HDB Friendly Faces, Lively Places Fund; HDB Lively Places Challenge; and URA's Our Favourite Place and Streets for People – merge to form the Lively Places Programme.

HDB shortens the balloting time for BTO flats from six weeks to three weeks. BTO projects will also be announced six months in advance, instead of three, to help home buyers better plan ahead.

HDB sets up the Home ownership Support Team (HST) to provide greater support to rental tenants, especially families with children, who are ready to buy a flat.

To encourage rental tenants to continue saving while working towards home ownership, HDB announces that rents would not increase for those who have made a down payment and signed the Agreement for Lease for a flat, even if their income increases.

HDB extends the Step-Up CPF Housing Grant to help second-timer lower-income families purchase 3-room resale flats in non-mature estates, and for second-timer families living in public rental flats to buy 2- or 3-room new or resale flats in non-mature estates.

The rules on CPF usage and HDB housing loan are updated to provide more flexibility for Singaporeans to buy a home, while safeguarding their retirement adequacy.

HDB introduces the open booking of flats, where home buyers are able to book from a pool of flats made available for sale all year round.

2020

HDB introduces a new Enhanced CPF Housing Grant (EHG) to make public housing more affordable and widen housing options for Singaporeans. The EHG extends to all eligible first-time home buyers – regardless of the purchase of a new or resale flat, the flat type, and location, and replaces the AHG and SHG. The income ceiling for EHG is set at $9,000 for families, and $4,500 for singles.

HDB raises the monthly household income ceiling for the purchase of flats from $12,000 to $14,000, and the income ceiling for the purchase of EC units from $14,000 to $16,000. The income ceiling for eligible singles aged 35 and above is also increased from $6,000 to $7,000.

HDB updates the use of 3D concrete printing to expand design capabilities and promote more sustainable construction. The largest 3D concrete printer in Southeast Asia is set up at its Centre of Building Research (CBR).

HDB reinforces its commitment to generate more clean energy with a new solar target of 540 MWp by 2030 – equivalent to powering 135,000 4-room flats with clean energy. The new target could ultimately generate 648 GWh of clean energy, potentially reducing carbon emissions by 324,000 tonnes per year.

HDB announces a new flat typology in Bukit Batok that caters to seniors. It will incorporate the concept of assisted living, where housing is integrated with care services.

Former Minister for National Development Mr Lawrence Wong announces that Bukit Merah, Queenstown, Choa Chu Kang, and Ang Mo Kio will be the next HDB towns to undergo the fourth series of the ROH programme.

To help buyers get their homes earlier, HDB announces it will do away with the ROF exercises, so that most of the unselected flats from the SBF exercises can be directly offered for open booking.

The maximum LBS bonus quantum for flat owners of 3-room or smaller flats, 4-room flats, and 5-room or larger flats increases by 50 percent to $30,000, $15,000, and $7,500 respectively.

ORGANISATIONAL AWARDS (2010 TO 2019)

2019

Council of Tall Buildings and Urban Habitat (CTBUH) Award 2019 – 10 Year Award – The Pinnacle@Duxton (International)

Council of Tall Buildings and Urban Habitat (CTBUH) Award 2019 – Best Tall Mixed-Use Building Category and Urban Habitat-Single Site Scale Category – Kampung Admiralty (International)

Excellence in Environmental Engineering and Science Honor Award (Small Projects Category) – Development of Floating Solar for use in Reservoir and Coastal Marine (International)

IES Prestigious Engineering Achievement Awards 2019, 2018, 2016, 2015, 2012, 2011 (8 Award Winners)

IFLA Asia-Pac Landscape Architecture Awards 2019, 2017, 2014 (2 Excellence, 4 Honourable Mention, 1 Merit Award Winners) (International)

MIPIM Asia Awards 2019 (Best Mixed-Use Development Category – Silver) – Oasis Terraces (International)

President's Science & Technology Award 2019 (PSTA) – Integrated Environmental Modeller

World Architecture Festival Awards 2019, 2018, 2016, 2015, 2010 (5 Award Winners) (International)

2018

BCA Built Environment Leadership Award (Platinum Star under Developer Category)

BCA Green Mark Platinum Champion Award

Singapore Quality Award (Special Commendation)

2017

American Environmental Sustainability Honor Award 2017 – A Biophilic MyWaterway@Punggol – Floating Wetlands and Freshwater-Tolerant Mangroves (International)

2016	Royal Institute of British Architects (RIBA) Award for International Excellence 2016 – SkyTerrace @ Dawson (International)
	The International Highrise Award 2016 (Special Recognition Award) – SkyVille @ Dawson (International)
	Geospatial Information Systems (GIS) Awards (Special Achievement) – Integrated Planning & Analysis (iPLAN) (International)
2013	American Society of Civil Engineers – Outstanding Civil Engineering Achievement Merit Award – My Waterway@Punggol (International)
	FIABCI Prix d'Excellence Award 2013 (Public Infrastructure Category – Gold) – My Waterway@Punggol (International)
	The International Architecture Award 2013 – My Waterway@Punggol (International)
2012	International Water Association (IWA) Global Superior Achievement Award & Global Grand Winner (Planning Category) – My Waterway@ Punggol (International)
	ASEAN Outstanding Engineering Achievement Award 2012 – My Waterway@Punggol
	Excellence in Environmental Engineering Award (Environmental Sustainability Category – Grand Prize Winner) – My Waterway@Punggol (International)
	Liveable Communities Award 2012 (Built Project Category – Gold) – My Waterway@Punggol (International)
2011	Urban Land Institute (ULI) Global Awards for Excellence and Awards for Excellence (Asia Pacific) – The Pinnacle@Duxton (International)
2010	Council of Tall Buildings and Urban Habitat (CTBUH) Award 2010 – Best Tall Building (Asia & Australasia) (International)
	2010 UN-Habitat Scroll of Honour Award (International)

Produced by

World Scientific Publishing Co. Pte. Ltd.
5 Toh Tuck Link, Singapore 596224

USA OFFICE: 27 Warren Street, Suite 401-402, Hackensack, NJ 07601
UK OFFICE: 57 Shelton Street, Covent Garden, London WC2H 9HE

HOME, TRULY
Building Dreams, Housing Hopes

ISBN 978-981-123-063-9 (hardcover)

Housing and Development Board

EDITORIAL TEAM: Randy Lim (Chairperson), Madhubala Balakrishna, Loh Swee Heng, Chan Lai Ching, Corrinne Lim, Eileen Neo, Foo-Ho Yoke Ming, Lee Sook Chin, Ng Yew Song, Raymond Tan, Tan Sze Tiong, Jeremiah Lim, Goh Keng Cheong, Shivvonne Wong, Eileen Lim, Chua Yeow Kheng, Jeremy Choy, Gary Wong, Chow Sue Ling, Lim Yi Han, Smita Wee

World Scientific

PROJECT MANAGER: Chua Hong Koon

EDITORS: Jiang Yulin, Daniele Lee

The Nutgraf

EDITOR: Sue-Ann Chia

WRITERS: Jacqueline Woo, Pearl Lee, Justin Kor, Derek Wong

PHOTOGRAPHERS: Sam Chin, Sean Lee, Lim Weixiang

DESIGNED BY

Redbean De Pte Ltd

National Library Board, Singapore Cataloguing in Publication Data

Names: Singapore. Housing and Development Board, editor. | The Nutgraf (Firm), editor.
Title: Home, truly : building dreams, housing hopes.
Description: Singapore : World Scientific Publishing Co. Pte. Ltd., [2020] | "Housing and Development Board"--Title page verso. | "The Nutgraf"--Title page verso.
Identifiers: OCN 1196336157 | ISBN 978-981-123-063-9 (hardcover)
Subjects: Public housing--Singapore--21st century. | Housing policy--Singapore--21st century. | Singapore. Housing and Development Board.
Classification: DDC 363.585095957--dc23

Printed in Singapore, 2020

The Housing and Development Board
would like to thank all residents
and partners whose contributions
helped make this book possible.

Photographs Courtesy of

Sembcorp Industries (page 33)
NTUC Health and the Housing and Development Board (pages 70 and 71)
Ministry of National Development (page 151)
Municipal Services Office (page 156)
National Archives of Singapore (pages 190, 192, and 197)
Ministry of Culture (page 191)
Ministry of Information, Communications and the Arts (page 203)
Ministry of Information and the Arts (pages 191, 192, 193, and 194)